Liz Fraser

...and other characters

Liz Fraser

...and other characters

My Autobiography

SIGNUM BOOKS

First published in Great Britain in 2012 by Signum Books,
an imprint of
Flashpoint Media Ltd
22 Signet Court
Cambridge
CB5 8LA

A CIP catalogue record for this book is available from the British Library.

ISBN 978 0 9566534 1 3

Editor: Jonathan Rigby
Designer: Peri Godbold
Managing Editor: Marcus Hearn

Printed and bound by CPI Group (UK) Ltd, Croydon, CR0 4YY.

For my mother
who worked her socks off to give me a good start,

and my dear father
whose life was ended too soon.

Contents

Preface

It was originally suggested that I call this book *Adventures of a Carry On Girl.*

"Leave that to the obituary columns," I said. "I'll wait till then."

In the meantime, I'd like everyone to know, if nothing else, that I once had dinner with Judy Garland.

Was that the most important thing that happened in my life?

Well, no.

But it's not bad for starters...

CHAPTER ONE

Over the Shop

I was born on the 14th of August 1930 in Southwark, near the Elephant and Castle, opposite a pub called The Rising Sun.

Thus I am an octogenarian. I used to find it funny when, on meeting husband-and-wife film producers Peter Rogers and Betty Box at various functions, they'd both say, "I'm 80 now, you know!" And I'd say, "Never! Good gracious, you look wonderful." Now when I tell people that I'm over 80 they seem surprised I'm not older.

Anyway, I was christened Elizabeth Joan Winch but known as Betty. Though if my *cousin* Betty was around I was stuck with the name Lulu.

Mother owned a shop at 165 Harper Road, just off the New Kent Road. It was a small place but sold everything that Tesco might have and more. Bags of coal, bundles of wood, sweets, gherkins, soft drinks and, in a small glass cabinet, first aid plasters, cough mixtures, medicines and Aspirin. Behind the counter were the cigarettes. Woodbines could be sold singly, as indeed were eggs. ("Only one please, Mrs Winch.") Blocks of ice were delivered every morning (no electricity – no freezer!) and Mother would chip away at them to keep the huge hams cool, which she'd cooked and then carved on a big china plate.

Fresh buns were delivered, too. She'd ice them, sprinkle hundreds and thousands over them and sell them for a ha'penny instead of a farthing. That's 100 per cent profit. Though I suspect most of the profits were drunk by my brother Philip in Tizer and eaten by me in gherkins.

Mother's day would start once the fresh bread had been delivered. It was called the Nine O'Clock Shop because she opened at 7.30 in the morning and the shutters were only pulled down at nine in the evening.

The wonder of it is that I never appreciated just how hard she worked; in retrospect, I wish I had. But you take everything for granted when you're small.

Behind the shop was a small back room. Sideboard, a table and chairs pushed against the wall, one armchair and an upright piano. Stairs leading to three small bedrooms. The lav was outside, next to the out-house, where there was a sink (cold water only), a mangle, a washing board and a stove. This is where the flat iron would be placed, and the ironing board was up all the time. Gas light only. Long tapers to turn on the gas taps. And in our back room, of course, the gas fire. We weren't poor, though. In fact, running a shop was considered middle class.

Mother's shop was part of a little row fronting a block of houses. There was also a gentlemen's barbers and, next door to that, a ladies' hairdressers. Inevitably there was a fish and chip shop too, where a friend of mine called Rita lived. Mother could always tell when I'd been playing over there because my nice new clothes reeked of fish.

Our next door neighbour on one side was a newsagents run by two little spinsters. On the other side there was a private house belonging to an Italian family. I'd climb onto a box on our side of the fence and Mrs Fiore would hand over huge plates of spaghetti; I've never tasted spaghetti as good as hers since. And the coffee stall outside the Elephant and Castle underground station was owned by another neighbour, a Mr Cole. I lived on their saveloys – at least two a day.

But it's the smells of the Elephant and Castle that linger longest in my memory. The farriers with their aroma of sizzling horses' hooves, the little hut where they cured kippers, the shop where they brewed sarsaparilla. Smells that have vanished from the London of today.

* * *

My father was 12 years younger than my mother and was a travelling salesman for a brewery, representing all the greyhound tracks – New Cross, Deptford, Stamford Bridge etc.

Going to the tracks was something we did as a family; it was part of our family make-up, really. We all went – even Mother on rare occasions, which was very unlike her. As a toddler I'd have a meat pie and with my pocket money I'd place little bets for sixpence each way. I'd do all the forecasts, too – "Six the field, please!"

The grounds were really beautiful. Grass tracks, flowers, floodlights, and the dogs parading in a central ring, coming on after a fanfare and sometimes even fireworks. I loved the colours of the dogs' jackets – red for track one, blue for track two, white for track three. Track four was black, track five orange and track six black-and-white. I simply loved the dogs and those memories remain among my happiest.

We had no shortage of pets at home. In fact, we owned a lame, retired greyhound called Janie, who'd been brought back by my father and lived the life of Riley for her declining years. We also had a tame chicken, Billy, who slept on Janie's back; a tortoise called Norman in the back yard; and a goldfish, name of Cyril, who lived happily with us for years and years. On top of all that we had a cat called Ollie, which my father would call by whistling 'The Waltz of the Cuckoos', the theme from the Laurel and Hardy films. Dad would whistle this tune and Ollie would come running for his food.

Because my mother worked so hard in the shop it was my father who took me everywhere. He was my world. Every Sunday we went off either to Petticoat Lane or East Lane just off the Walworth

Road. My best coat and matching hat would be worn. We'd go to little dress shops and pick up new outfits for me – invariably in pink with velvet collars and a hat to match. Dad would have cockles or whelks and I'd have my glass of sarsaparilla and a penny bag of chestnuts (when in season) or an ice cream cone from a stall. In the afternoons we'd go up West and listen to the brass bands on the Embankment. Then in the evenings the whole family would play a card game called Nap, which stood me in good stead when I later developed a taste for bridge.

As a family we'd eat fish on Fridays and pie, liquor and mash on Saturdays. And on my Sunday trips with Dad he'd buy live eels off a stall, with me looking the other way. They'd wriggle around until the chopper came down. Then they'd be put out in pots and topped with jelly. To this day I've never tasted one. The whole spectacle put me off for life. I wouldn't eat chicken either – not for years. Just in case it was our Billy!

Every Wednesday evening my father would take me to the South London Palace, which was my weekly treat. It was just past the Elephant and Castle Tube, near the coffee stall run by Mr and Mrs Cole. I loved the theatre atmosphere and got to see all the greats of variety – Wilson, Keppel and Betty, George Formby, Max Miller, The Crazy Gang.

There'd be a special variety show for children on Wednesdays and there was always a bit where a spotlight would roam around the audience. Whichever child it landed on would be invited up on stage. One time it landed on me and I was given a present by the man on stage. What a tale to tell Mum! That man, by the way, was Tommy Trinder, a great comedian of times past whom I'd meet again many years later – on some radio panel game, I think.

* * *

I only learned years later that Father was actually my mother's second husband. She'd been married to a young Irishman called

McGoldrick who died at the age of 21. I only found this out after my mother died, through a memorial card contained in a little box. There was also a rosary in it. Whether or not my brother had known this at an early age I don't know. He was 11 years my senior and it was only during the war, when I addressed letters to him as Philip Winch instead of Philip McGoldrick, that I found out he was actually my half-brother.

All our relatives lived around Southwark, Deptford and Lewisham. My grandparents were all dead; in fact, I discovered that my mother's father had committed suicide in Deptford Canal. Her family originally came from Kent and now and again we'd visit my Uncle Harry, Auntie Nance and cousin Harold in Deptford. They had an upright piano and it seemed as if the whole family could sing, especially at Christmas time. Back then Nellie Dean always seemed to be dreaming by the old mill stream – Auntie Nance knew all those songs that these days are only heard at old-time music halls. But Uncle Harry was the real showman. He'd do magic tricks. The wonder of it!

Harry was Mother's older brother. The second son, Nippy, was a bookie's runner. Betting was illegal then, so the runner would stand on a street corner and write people's bets on a little pad while keeping an eye out for policemen. I'd sometimes earn a couple of pennies from being the 'eyes' for the bookie's runner. All the local kids did. We'd spot a policeman, run to the bookie and he'd scarper. Uncle Nippy was a runner all his life and kept his six children well fed and clothed.

Holidays were important. Auntie and her family from Deptford would go down to Kent to pick hops. 'Hopping' was a popular holiday for cockneys; it was hard work but got you away from London and into the countryside. Our family, however, would go to Ramsgate, and for day trips Father would take me to Brighton, which I loved. Sometimes we even went as far afield as the Isle of Wight.

One day, on one of our many seaside excursions, Father took me walking along the sea front and we came across a stall selling pictures a man had painted with his feet. He had no hands so he'd taught himself to write and draw with his feet. I became determined to teach myself to do the same. I had a lively imagination and thought that if I was ever kidnapped, and my hands were tied, this would be a useful skill to have. So I'd pick up a pencil between my big toe and second toe and write "I've been kidnapped!" or "Help me!" in big letters. I became quite adept at this but unfortunately I was never kidnapped.

In those days all the kids played games in the street. There weren't many cars around so it was quite safe. Hide and seek, hopscotch, marbles (gorgeous colours), skipping, hoops. Actually, I wasn't much good at that last one. My favourite was called 'undercoats', in which we all piled our coats in the middle of the road and crawled under them. This one wasn't popular with my mother, though, especially if I was wearing my 'best'. I also vaguely remember running through the streets shouting "Tommy Farr!" I realised later that he was a well-known boxer, though at the time I probably only called out his name because all the other kids did.

My nearest playground was just down the road from the abattoir. Swings with no bars, slides which you could fall from (and did). No health and safety in those days! Just some iodine and a plaster to cover the wound when you got back home. Now and again a roundabout would appear on the street pulled by a horse; for a ha'penny we could clamber on and the man would spin us round.

Ice cream treats were reliant on a man on a bicycle with an icebox on his back. He'd ring a bell and we'd all go rushing to get a cornet.

Street parties were frequent. The King's Silver Jubilee in 1935 was the best one I can remember. Rows and rows of streets with bunting and flags hung from the windows, plus long trestles and chairs for us kids and everyone doing the cakes and jellies and whatever. I remember that very well. Strange, how some memories are forever stamped in your head yet other important things are difficult to recall.

* * *

When I was seven my mother was taken off by ambulance to Guy's Hospital, where she nearly died of a burst appendix. My father was already in hospital with a bad chest, which would turn out to be TB. I was looked after by Mr and Mrs Cole and by Philip, who by then had started work as a window-dresser at the wonderful Fortnum & Mason. I was sleepwalking, apparently, and strangely enough the Coles thought there was nothing unusual about this. Philip knew better, however, so I was taken round the corner to the doctor's in New Kent Road.

It turned out I was seriously ill with mastoids (or whatever it's called now), so I was hastily admitted to Brooke Street Hospital and a deep infection was operated on behind my ear. So there we were, three Winches, all confined to London's finest medical institutions – and all in the same week! It was hard on Philip as he was only in his late teens at the time and had to visit all three of us in our different hospitals. In fact, my father discharged himself from hospital in order to take care of me. In retrospect this was a serious mistake given his own poor health; he never fully recovered after that.

While in hospital in 1937 I'd buy the *Daily Mirror* from the newspaper trolley every day. (I'm an avid newspaper reader even now and buy at least two different papers a day.) I'd loved reading from at least the age of five and had my own library card for the Bricklayers Arms Library. I'd also go to a bookshop on Tower Bridge Road where you could borrow books for a tiny sum and pay for another on return. Once I'd grown out of Enid Blyton I went on to the Just William books and finally graduated to Ethel M Dell, reading all about romantic sheikhs and such like. No *Fifty Shades of Grey* back then!

When we were all out of our various hospitals, life went happily on – my brother at Fortnum's, my dad at the race track, my mother in her shop and me learning joined-up writing at Harper Road School round the corner. It was just an ordinary run-of-the-mill school; we all had our separate desks and we had to listen and had to learn.

There were also plenty of cinemas – at least four – that you could visit with or without parents. I was forbidden to go to the 'fleapit' but we all went in now and then. On Saturday mornings at the Elephant and Castle Trocadero there was the Cinema Club for unaccompanied children. The aisles would be jammed with hundreds of us, all tumbling and screaming to get to the best seats, then piping down as we watched the latest episode of *Flash Gordon*. The cartoons were wonderful – we all loved the black-and-white mouse getting the better of the black-and-white cat. Everything was black-and-white then, of course.

Saturday evenings at the Trocadero were the best, because the programme included an amateur talent show. Whoever got the most applause would win a prize and then everyone would settle down for the main feature. At the ABC, however, the entertainment would start even before you got into the cinema. As you waited in line buskers would dance and sing and then go round with a cup for money. One of them became quite a celebrity. 'Old Mutton Eye' had one good eye and one bad eye and played both the accordion and a collapsible piano. I heard years later that he'd apparently become quite rich on the proceeds.

* * *

The end for us as a family came in September 1939.

War had no significance for me at that age, but my family would all be glued to the accumulator radio that sat on our kitchen table. I had just had my ninth birthday when the whatsit hit the fan. So, without really understanding what was happening, I was sent with my whole school to Kent. I was armed with a small suitcase and had a box with a gas mask in it strapped over my shoulder. I was also dressed to the nines, of course, in a pink coat with a velvet collar. The scene at the railway station was a bit like St Trinian's really – everyone screaming and shouting, and nobody really appreciating that we were leaving our parents behind.

What an adventure!

We were deposited in a school hall at Crockham Hill in Kent. In we all piled, still not really knowing what was happening. Standing there with name labels safety-pinned to our coats – Betty Winch.

We weren't allocated at random. People came in and looked us up and down, choosing whomever they liked the look of best. Fortunately, I was picked out immediately; it was the pink coat, I expect. I didn't realise how lucky I was (who would at the age of nine?) but a lady called Lilly chose me, together with a pair of twins and another, slightly older girl called Doris Collins.

We were taken away in a car! We peered out of the window at an approaching gate, then swept past a long line of trees (a drive!) with a beautiful big house at the end. This was Northfield, Chartwell, Westerham, Kent.

A childless couple, Mr and Mrs Salisbury, had given Lilly the task of picking up four cockney kids for them to look after. Lilly was their housekeeper and was married to the chauffeur, and the pair of them lived in their own cottage on the estate.

I'll never forget being taken to the Blue Room, which was to be mine. It looked like the set of a Shirley Temple film, which was very exciting to me as I was a big fan of hers. The others all had their own rooms too, all named after different colours. Lilly unpacked everything and there I was – in a beautiful house surrounded by lawns and a lake.

Two cars, a chauffeur, housekeeper, gardener and cook. Flowers in all rooms, including orchids from the greenhouse (I'd never seen one before). Electricity! Music boxes, including one that doubled as a cigarette box. A bunker that was built into one wall, with a long passage leading to rooms at the far end – and stocked with as many goods as Mother's shop. Food came from Fortnum's and I became accustomed to a life of luxury... I was Betty in Wonderland.

Unbeknown to me at the time, the neighbouring estate belonged to a Mr and Mrs Winston Churchill. Later, Mr Churchill came to visit us evacuees. A big, cigar-smoking person. We all liked him; in fact, I often used to sit on his knee. We were allowed to walk round Chartwell and pick up acorns for his pigs. I also met his daughter Sarah.

School at Crockham Hill was a shock, however. The kids were still writing in capitals and we from Southwark were all doing joined-up writing. So we all had to back-track to their standards. In fact, jumping ahead a bit, when I did return home I was way behind my age group. More on that when I'm older.

When Father visited me from London, I imagine he was quite shocked by all the luxury. But, along with our teachers, he began to worry that Kent was vulnerable to bombing. As an entire school we were therefore re-evacuated to a village in Devon – Chudleigh. Population of about a couple of thousand, I should think.

So it was goodbye to the Salisburys. I kept in touch with them long after the war. Mrs Salisbury became a widow but I maintained contact with her until her death. I actually visited the house about five years ago. I 'gatecrashed', following a milk van through the electric gates and into the drive. The owners were very kind and let me peer around what had once been a part of my life. It now has an underground swimming pool to die for – especially me, as I can't swim.

* * *

So we were all lined up once again, with labels re-attached, in the church hall at Chudleigh. Presumably because I was still dressed in the pink coat with the velvet collar, I was pretty much the first to be picked – along with a girl called Pam – by the district nurse. She then drove us for what seemed like 40 miles. Finally we passed a small house (the lodge), went down a mile-long drive and came to a magnificent red-brick building at the end – Whiteway House, owned by the Farquhars. It was as if we'd come home to Tara from *Gone with the Wind*.

The district nurse went round the building to a courtyard with two cottages. Pam and I were staying with the chauffeur, who drove the two Daimlers. Mr and Mrs Fairbrother were probably in their early sixties. They had no children and I think it was 'the big house' that decided they should take us on as their contribution to the war effort. But how wonderful they were to us. It must have been difficult for them – after all, they'd led a quiet life and suddenly there were two nine-year-olds running around.

And run we did. We had acres to play in, horses, chickens, dogs, cows etc to look at, and an outdoor swimming pool (again, only to look at). There was even a peacock strutting round the grounds, and when his tail was feathered out it was like the eighth wonder of the world.

We were four and a half miles from the village and the school. Every day we walked there and back – idyllic. Picking wild strawberries, nuts, flowers... I loved it. And sometimes I'd stop halfway at a solitary farm where there were two good-looking boys to talk to. It's hard to explain how odd it all seemed and yet how quickly I took to it.

It was 1941 now, and my father came to see me as often as possible. My mother was unable to leave the shop, ever. Pam's mother, however, wanted her to go back to London, despite the air raids. So I was happily left behind with 'Uncle' and 'Auntie', playing cards and eating tons of Devonshire cream – cream on bread at both breakfast and tea-time! (The cottage next door housed the cow man and his wife, the dairy maid.) I had my own kitten (feral), pinched by me from a litter that was being culled – or shot, to be blunt. And I sometimes had play time in the Daimler, which had a phone from the back seat to the driver. I loved it all.

Things changed, however. Suddenly the penny dropped among the 'authorities' that there was this poor little girl (me) who was walking nine miles a day, alone. So it was decided I should be relocated to the village. But where could they put me?

June, my best friend at the school, said her mother would have me. I asked the people in charge if I could stay with June and her mother and younger brother, and they agreed. But no cat. So I left her behind, never to have a cat again.

Without wanting to give away the plot, I slept in the same bed with June and her brother. Her mother, you see, had lots of 'uncles' who came and went and slept in her room. I was so lucky to have so many uncles! But I looked forward to the day when my father was due to see me in my new home. And see me he did. I wasn't looking too good, with scabies all over my face, and within the hour he had me out of that place, telling the authorities that he didn't appreciate the fact that I was housed with the village prostitute.

So, with my father staying on, another Auntie and Uncle had to be found. This latest move was to the edge of the village and to yet another childless couple. (No coincidence, surely? Three out of three.) Mr and Mrs Burnett were lovely; they had a bungalow, went to chapel and made lots of wonderful cakes in tins. Uncle was the ARP Warden and had to learn all the silhouettes of enemy aeroplanes. I learned them too. Heaven help the Junkers and Stukas etc if they flew past me!

The headmaster of the church school didn't bother much with education. He had a market garden and all the schoolchildren had to pick flowers and bunch them up for sale. Didn't seem a bad idea to us illiterate kids who still weren't doing joined-up writing. But the little school also put on lots of shows in which we all sang and danced. I performed well-known monologues, which I suppose was the beginning of a life-long career. There were twin sisters from London who tap-danced together but their ten-year-old lives were cut short by polio. Another forgotten illness; just think of all those cemeteries where there are no people over 50.

My father was now in a sanatorium but I didn't understand what that meant. I'd write to him, so I knew his address had changed. But I was too young to realise what was happening. I recently discovered one of his last letters to my mother, sent from the Royal National Sanatorium in Bournemouth (ward six) and bearing a tuppenny stamp.

> To my dearest wife
> Thanks for your letter. I'm glad to know of your early and safe arrival.
> It is the most memorable morning – brilliant sunshine, wonderful blue sky, birds outside all chirping away. A robin was outside a little while ago. In fact, it is absolutely glorious.
> I want to thank you, darling, for the wonderful happy years of life you have given to me, and may we have many more anniversaries to celebrate in the proper manner.
> I shall see your sweet face on Sunday, of course.
> God bless you always
> Your loving hubby

The last time I saw my father was when he had me moved away from the village tart. When the train taking him back to London disappeared from view in March 1942, I didn't realise that his goodbye kiss would be forever. He died in May, aged 40; I was just 11. He was the love of my life.

The headmaster told me the news and it broke my heart. In assembly the whole school sang 'Abide With Me' as a tribute to my father. To this day I can't hear that hymn without crying.

* * *

Life was hard for my mother, alone, with a son in the Army and me in Devon. She eventually gave in to my pleading to come home, so some months later I returned to London – to my mother, the Anderson Shelter, the buzz bombs and the V2s. The city I had known was in ruins and it was shocking to see.

When my mother and father were still together they used to shelter down the Elephant and Castle Tube, or sometimes Piccadilly Circus if they were lucky. Piccadilly had the deepest tunnel and they were packed in down there like sardines. By the time I returned home, though, Mother had the Anderson Shelter in the garden. We slept in there every night and as I was asthmatic I'd wheeze away on my camp-bed.

The air raid sirens were a constant and dreadful sound, signalling the arrival of bombing planes or buzz bombs. These pilot-less, cross-shaped weapons flew over the coast and countryside with an indescribable deep-throated 'grrrrr' sound. When they stopped 'buzzing' they were on their way down. The flying bomb was about to hit and blow all and sundry to smithereens. If the engine cut out directly above you it was safe; it would land elsewhere and the loud bang meant some other poor bastards had bought it. If the sound stopped further away there would be the terror of waiting to be blown up.

One morning we woke up and, leaving the Anderson Shelter, found that there was acrid smoke pouring out of the house. To be exact, it was pouring out of my bedroom. During the night an incendiary bomb had come through the roof and landed on the floor by my bed. The ARP warden had put it out, but I was left with charred floorboards for the rest of my time at Harper Road so I moved into my brother's empty room. The bomb damage also left the shop without windows. The front had to be boarded up, all except for a small pane of glass with tape across it. But we were still in business.

When Philip came home on leave he'd pick up tins of beans and soup and pile them high, with just one can perched at the top, in the style he'd learned as a window-dresser at Fortnum & Mason. Though Mother praised these impressive pyramid displays, she became terrified of knocking the whole thing down whenever someone asked for something in the window. But he wouldn't listen, and I soon saw my mother's point of view when I was serving in the shop myself.

Someone would ask for Heinz Baked Beans and I'd look behind the counter and all round the shop and say, "I'm sorry, we don't have any."

"Yes, you have," the customer would reply. "You've got about 50 tins of it in the window!"

And I'd have to crawl under and get one. Quite often the whole lot would come down. I should have got danger money!

* * *

When I came back to London I also went straight back to Harper Road School round the corner. Amazing to think how many evacuees were returned to their homes while the war was still raging. Nearby was St Saviour's and St Olave's Grammar School for Girls in the New Kent Road. We tearaway kids would laugh at the grammar school pupils in their straw hats and matching skirts and blazers. "Old four-eyes!" we'd shout to any of them wearing glasses. "Old rotten-hat!" we'd yell at the others. Great fun.

"I'm sending you to that school," my mother said one day.

I was horrified and refused. I thought I'd win as she'd never been strict with me. But she realised that my education had suffered while I was away so she made an appointment to see the headmistress. On her afternoon off she virtually dragged me to the school. She was paying for me (no scholarship for this illiterate scumbag), and I was accepted.

I could either be in a class with my own age group and catch up on a year's Latin, French and Algebra (what?), or I could go to a younger class and start at the beginning.

"I'll catch up," I said.

But I never did – 'parlez-vous' and 'dominum dominorum' were forever alien to me. However, my joined-up writing was OK and I fell in love with Miss Cager, the English teacher, eventually leaving St Saviour's with an A+ in Literature and an A in Grammar. Top of the class!

I was there from the ages of 13 to 17. The school I had dreaded was really the making of me. We had assembly every morning (with hymns) and would then rush off to our classes. It was certainly strict – eating on the streets in uniform brought an immediate detention. And it was a super place to receive a first-class education. So thank you, mum. And thank you to all those dedicated teachers, too.

Our playing fields were in Dulwich. Cricket or tennis – we had to choose. We all loved the wonderful cricket teacher, Miss Robinson, so everyone elected to be cricketers. I was 'wicket' and I loved it. According to Miss Robinson, the selection committee for the England women's cricket team had their eye on me. The only trouble with all this was that upon leaving there was never a cry of "Anyone for cricket?" My wicket-keeping talents were wasted and to this day I cannot play tennis. However, my cricketing prowess did help me to get the part of Cynthia Kite in the Boultings' film *I'm All Right Jack*.

More on that later.

CHAPTER TWO

So Long As It's Brighton

Drama was high on the agenda at school, and in addition I attended Goldsmiths College in the evenings.

As a 14-year-old I joined the drama group there and played the 12-year-old 'ghost' child in J M Barrie's *Dear Brutus*. Goldsmiths was quite an exclusive establishment so the show was reviewed in both the *South London Press* and *Lewisham Times*. I got great notices. The director, Catherine Malt, recommended that when I left school I should try for a drama scholarship at the London School of Dramatic Art.

My ambition to go on the stage received a particularly negative reaction from my brother Philip.

"Well," he said, "who's going to keep you?"

"Don't worry," I replied, "you'll never have to keep me. I'll make my own way, thank you very much."

After leaving St Saviour's I attended the City of London College for Commerce, Book-Keeping, Shorthand and Typing, which gave me a working knowledge of the Stock Exchange that was to serve me well in later life. I graduated with 145 shorthand and 80 typing – which means nothing nowadays, of course, but back then it enabled me to get all the highest paid secretarial jobs.

I also did as Catherine Malt suggested and won an evening scholarship to the London School of Dramatic Art for two years, which was perfect for me. I did temporary work as a shorthand typist during the day and studied in the evening – walking home every night after ten o'clock from Elephant and Castle Tube, about a mile or so. Not today I wouldn't!

The school was run by an elderly lady called Gertrude Pickersgill and I loved my time there. I even got to play Cordelia in *King Lear*. (That would never happen again.) At the end of the two years we had our leaving show at the Portland Hall, in which each student had to perform three pieces (drama, comedy, and mime) in front of various artists' agents.

It was July 1952 and the adjudicator was the top casting director Weston Drury, who announced at the end that he was giving me first place for drama. "Unfortunately," he added, "this student has no sense of comedy." In fact, he placed me last in that category.

Afterwards, I was approached by a man who introduced himself as Kenneth Seale.

"I'm the editor of *Spotlight*," he said. I must have looked completely blank because he added, "The casting directory." He went on to say he completely disagreed with Weston Drury's opinion. "I thought your comedy was excellent."

"Thank you very much," I replied, not really thinking too much about it.

Also that day, I won the Michael Redgrave Prize for mime. I was presented with the book *Building a Character* by Constantin Stanislavski, inscribed "with congratulations and best wishes" by Michael Redgrave himself. I felt very proud. I wrote to thank him and still have his reply.

I still have the book, too. I've looked after it very well but have never read it!

* * *

Temporary typing for three days a week helped me pay my way and the other two I spent trawling the theatrical agencies for work. I was employed at a firm called Muller and Phipps, just off Park Lane, and was in great demand because of my typing speed. I worked very hard to keep it up, peaking at 85 words a minute, and my fingers would ache at the end of each day. I'd regularly manage to type ten letters in the same time it took other secretaries to type one.

I was even offered a post as PA to the Member of Parliament for Rotherham. But the clatter of my typewriter was just a pretence, really. I had no desire to be a secretary full time. Remembering Philip's words, I was determined that I would never need to be 'kept' and so made sure to give my mother four pounds a week.

I then put an advertisement in *The Stage*. "Drama student just finished and would appreciate any work in a repertory company," it read.

I had three replies. Two involved paying to work (!) and the third was from the repertory company at Accrington – to be an ASM (Assistant Stage Manager and small parts) for £4-10s a week. As I was getting about £6-10s as a typist this was quite a drop. But the money didn't matter. I wanted to act.

My digs (bed, breakfast, dinner) cost £2-10s a week and I played my very first part as the maid in *Jane Eyre*. I made my first entrance carrying a coal scuttle. I was so nervous it rattled. I was in charge of props and furniture, so I got to know all the local shopkeepers, who lent us all sorts of things. As a result, the set for *Jane Eyre* looked wonderful. I also arranged for free hairdressing and cinema tickets for the cast.

I worked in Accrington for three months, acted a couple of times, and fell for the leading man – Richard Butler. I inadvertently upset him a few times, though.

When he was playing Rochester in *Jane Eyre*, it happened to be Wakes Week, meaning all the shops were closed. So how to get milk for the tea that Richard drank on stage? I wanted the scene to look realistic when the tea was poured out, so I mixed water with a little paint to make it look milky. Unfortunately, I forgot to warn Richard not to actually *drink* the tea.

"What was in that milk jug?" he yelled as he came tearing off stage. "I've been poisoned, for Christ's sake! What the hell *was* that?"

"It was only water paint," I stammered.

Well, this was Act One and he refused to go on again for Act Two until he'd heard from a doctor that he'd be OK. So I ran out of the stage door, waited for a few minutes, then went back in, puffing and panting. I'd had a word with the local doctor, I said, and apparently drinking water paint was nothing to worry about. And so Richard went back on.

The following week I blundered again during *Murder at the Vicarage*, in which Richard played the vicar. I was sitting backstage and was so besotted with Richard that I didn't realise I'd failed to ring the telephone bell at the appropriate time. Richard ad-libbed for a bit, then decided to just pick up the receiver and start talking. It was at this point that I woke up and finally rang the bell, which was a bit embarrassing for Richard as he was already speaking on the phone.

"Good Lord, Marjorie," he improvised. "There must be some sort of fault on the line. Can you hear ringing?"

Despite these problems, I left with a written reference; the director had been particularly impressed by all the lovely furniture I'd rounded up for *Jane Eyre*, but didn't mention my acting! Full of confidence, I decided pantomime would be next.

* * *

Rosamund Leslie, a friend from drama school, was set to be in the chorus of *Babes in the Wood* at the Brighton Hippodrome, with Arthur Askey as Dame. So, through sheer ignorance, I went to the company's head office in the Aldwych and asked to see the well-known impresario Frank Marshall, who was putting all the pantos on in about half-a-dozen different venues.

I joined a group waiting in his office who, unbeknown to me, were all there to be seen as principal girls and boys. (Females played both.) When my turn came I got to see the great man himself.

"Boy or girl?" he asked.

"Hmm, I don't mind," I said, "so long as it's Brighton." Of course, I had no right to be seeing him at all. "I'm an actress," I explained, "and my friend has got into the chorus at Brighton."

This mistake amused him, so he told me he was seeing principals that afternoon at the Drury Lane Theatre and would hear me sing for the chorus at the same time. I had a little black book of agents with me, so I looked in it for anyone who gave singing lessons. I bought the sheet music for 'It's a Lovely Day Today' from *Call Me Madam*, phoned a singing teacher from a red telephone box and booked a 30-minute session, which was all I had the money for.

Well, "IT'S a lovely day" is a very high note to start on. Two lines were all I could get through and I knew I had to take a deep breath to get the "It's" out. After the singing lesson, I arrived at this magnificent theatre where, in a large side room, a lot of tall, willowy girls in leotards and tights were making a cacophony of high notes. They all had song portfolios with them, whereas I just had my single sheet. I could hear what was happening on stage through the tannoy system; a girl with a really beautiful voice was singing 'Ave Maria'. I felt the need to explain my presence so I told all and sundry that I was just there for the chorus.

"Miss Winch!" was called.

Onto this huge stage I went, clutching my single sheet of music. Just a piano in the centre and bright lights. The pianist took the sheet and started the first note.

"That's too high," I whispered.

After several attempts at a lower note I'd more or less got out "It's a lovely day" when a voice from the darkness said, "OK. You can go to Leicester."

"But I wanted to go to Brighton with my friend," I said.

I remember hearing laughter from the auditorium at that.

"All right, Brighton," came the response – and that was it!

When you know nothing you're afraid of nothing. The sheer cheek of my ignorance gave me a chance that hundreds of singers and dancers would have given their eye-teeth for.

Several weeks later I went to Drury Lane again to start rehearsals for *Babes in the Wood*. There were 24 of us in the chorus (the shows were really huge in those days), and in no time at all it became obvious that I couldn't dance. So the other 23 girls worked their ballet shoes off while I ran on as a robin downstage left with my head down and my wings spread out.

In the second week of rehearsals we started on the songs. One of them concluded on a very high note and I just mimed it.

"Why did you mime?" asked our choreographer, Deirdre Vivian.

"I can't sing," I replied.

"You can't sing and you can't dance! How come you're here?"

"Oh," I replied, "I'm an actress!"

So that was that. Everybody else sang and danced, and I thoroughly enjoyed my first attempt at a musical, doing neither.

* * *

In Brighton I shared digs with my friend Rosamund and was paid £6 per week. You received another £2 if you could fly on a wire but unfortunately I was too heavy! The drummer I stood in front of in my beak and wings would write me funny notes to make me laugh. And Arthur Askey thought I was a hoot. (Couldn't sing or dance!) I'd often have tea with him and was to meet him again several times in my future career.

The following year I worked on a second Frank Marshall pantomime, in the chorus again. This time it was *Cinderella* at the Leicester Palace. I was with another drama school friend, Enid Cassin (who really *was* a singer), and we'd spotted some nice-sounding digs advertised in *The Stage*. They were £4-15s a week. We were only on £6 but thought it would be worth it. As far as we were concerned we were actresses, not chorus.

The landlords were a Mr and Mrs Joyce. Their visitors' book in the hall had been signed by every star you could think of. Bonar Colleano and Susan Shaw had been in just the previous week!

So they weren't best pleased when they found out we were only chorus. Nor was Jane Martin, who was in the same digs and was playing Cinderella.

Before leaving for Leicester, I'd made a point of going to see her in the touring production of *Carousel.* I went round afterwards to say how good she was; after all, we were due to be working together *and* sharing digs. I knocked on her dressing room door and a melodious voice from inside called, "Come in!"

In I went. "Oh, Miss Martin," I said, "I thought you were ever so good."

"Oh, thank you," she said. "Do I know you?"

"Well, actually, we're sharing digs in Leicester for the pantomime season so I thought I'd just come along and say hello."

"Oh really?" she said. "What part are you playing?"

"Oh, I'm in the chorus."

Long pause. She then turned her back on me and continued removing her make-up. She didn't say another word. The same was true in Leicester. In fact, she not only insisted on using the bathroom first every morning but also refused to eat with Enid and me. As a result, we had to have our breakfast at a very early hour.

During the run we discovered that Mr Joyce had changed the light bulb in our bedroom, and when we complained that we couldn't read by a 40-watt bulb he and his wife decided they'd had enough of us chorus girls. We came back to the digs that night to find our suitcases on the pavement. There was no other accommodation to be had by then so we had to share rooms and beds with other members of the chorus. When he heard about what had happened, the company manager had the Joyces removed from the theatre's digs list.

Anyway, after this experience poor Enid gave up the theatre immediately. She went on to help set up the Press Council and had a wonderful career, with chauffeur-driven cars and everything.

* * *

When not working I'd still do secretarial work on odd days for an income. I paid for professional photos and visited all the agencies to get work. As a result I found myself touring a lot of the time.

My first tour came in between my two Frank Marshall pantomimes in 1953. It was a dreadful play called *One Way Traffic*. It had quite a large cast and my first boyfriend, Graham Armitage, was the juvenile lead. Graham and I would just hold hands together, and I realised that the profession my mother had worried about me going into was actually very nice. After all, when saying good night Graham would only kiss me on the cheek.

"Your boyfriend is queer!" announced the leading lady. Well, I didn't think he was odd at all so I told Graham what she'd said.

"Cheek!" he cried.

In London I met his flat-mate Alan. They had a small place near the Marylebone Road and, when Graham had to pop out to get some fish and chips, Alan turned to me and said, "I love him, you know. He won't ever marry *you*."

I told Graham about this as well and he just said "Cheek!" again.

So my first boyfriend was gay. I met him again years later when we did *Randall and Hopkirk (Deceased)* together and we both laughed about it. Sadly, he died back in 1999.

The traffic in *One Way Traffic* was sex traffic. I didn't understand it at all. It was all about six beauty queens who are exported to Egypt or somewhere to become harem girls for a rich sultan. We had a walking nude in it – and according to the Lord Chamberlain they had to stay absolutely still in those days. In fact, Phyllis Dixey was touring one of her nude pageant shows at the same time and was keeping strictly to the rules.

A strange thing happened at the end of our week in Exeter. The next date was Tonypandy, and when we got on the train we looked up and down for our carriage, which the producer always reserved for us in advance. But we couldn't find a sign for the *One Way Traffic* company anywhere. Eventually we found a label that read, 'The Road to Shame company – Exeter to Tonypandy'. For that

Tonypandy week, and that week only, the play's title had apparently been changed to *The Road to Shame*. Yet during that week we had lots of people turning up in the audience with babes in arms. There'd be mothers sitting in the front row with screaming kids, which was a bit strange to say the least.

When the play came to the Camberwell Palace (long gone now, like so many theatres), I booked seats for my mother and brother in the front row. At last we were near my home and they could see me on stage. But at half time, when I peered through the curtain to see them, their seats were empty. Later, Philip told me he'd had to take Mother home as the show was disgusting.

Of course, I hadn't realised there was anything untoward about this 'wonderful' play. But, to round off Act One, the walking nude came downstage, sat astride the leading man and wriggled about on top of him. After grunting a bit, he fell asleep and started snoring. Curtain. They don't make climaxes like that any more!

Frankly, I have no idea how the producer ever thought he'd get away with it. A representative from the Lord Chamberlain's office finally caught up with us in Leicester and immediately demanded that the play should be taken off. In the event, there was a compromise whereby our walking nude, Janey, took off fewer clothes (though she added more wriggling to compensate). And so the tour went on.

The production was a shambles most of the time, and as often as not the big dramatic moment at the very end didn't work. All six beauty queens have escaped being sold into white slavery and the villain of the piece is killed. "Ah, I've been shot!" he'd cry. Only the gun shot from off stage frequently didn't come. We'd hear this puny 'click' from the wings and realise that the prop revolver hadn't fired. So the villain would clutch his stomach, sink to the floor and say "Ah, I've been poisoned!" instead.

Very clever.

* * *

There were eight girls in the show and we all get on really well. One, Eugenie May, was later killed in a plane crash while en route to meet an Italian prince. Another, Ann Donati, subsequently married Tommy Steele.

It was during this tour that we girls went in for a bit of communing with the spirits. We'd spend most nights after the performance clustered round a planchette. I was quite interested in spiritualism and the supernatural; at that young age your mind is very open to it and mine was more open than most because I desperately wanted to believe it. It was over ten years since my father had died and I wanted very much to have a chat with him.

So we'd sit round this planchette and put our fingers on the top of an upturned glass. All the letters of the alphabet were scattered around, with cut-out letters spelling 'Yes' on one side and 'No' on the other.

At first I was quite sceptical, thinking that one or other of us was pushing the glass around deliberately. But no one would admit to it and things eventually became quite eerie. All these spirits would come through; my own personal spirit guide was called Cyril.

Then one night the letters spelled out "D-A-D."

"Dad?" we all said. "Whose dad?"

"Betty's dad," came the reply.

I was Elizabeth by now so I absolutely froze; none of the girls knew that I'd ever been called Betty. To confirm who it was, I asked what my mother's Christian name was.

"B-E-S-S-I-E."

He gave his love to us both and that was that. But I believed in it from that moment on and during that tour Father and I would chat quite frequently. One time I asked him to name the winner of the Derby, but it lost. "Well, I just fancied it," he said.

The strangest thing, though, was this. "You'll be cast in a play with Bebe Daniels and Ben Lyon," he said. (They were big stars at the time, thanks to their radio show *Life with the Lyons*.) "Go to see Harry Foster."

"Who's Harry Foster?" I asked.

"A-G-E-N-T."

Well, I'd never heard of Harry Foster but it turned out he was a really big agent who represented lots of major variety stars. So during one of our 'weeks out' I looked him up and went to his office in Piccadilly. He was very polite but said he didn't represent actors. I told him I wondered if there might be anything for me in the Bebe Daniels and Ben Lyon show. To my horror he nearly jumped on me, demanding to know how I knew. He was negotiating for a Bebe and Ben season at Blackpool but it was still very hush-hush.

My explanation was greeted with silence. He then said it was the strangest thing he'd ever heard and assured me that if the show came to pass I'd definitely be in it. Later he was kind enough to write to me to say the show had fallen through after all. He was sorry, he said, that my Dad had been wrong!

* * *

What with hanging around with Graham, communicating with my late father and chasing up potential work with Bebe Daniels in Blackpool, it seems as if I had an awful lot of spare time during that tour of *One Way Traffic*. As it turned out, all that spare time was to be a big problem for our producer – and it was me who eventually had to blow the whistle on him.

It transpired that we'd all been employed because we weren't yet members of Equity. Of course, the producer hadn't told Equity that he was using non-members but eventually an Equity representative paid us a visit on one of our tour dates. He told us that we were being paid much less than the Equity minimum, which was £6 a week at that time. We were on £3-10s.

He also pointed out that touring shows were only allowed to have a limited number of 'weeks out' so that the actors weren't left hanging around mid-tour, unpaid and waiting for the next tour date to begin. Again, none of us knew this, which was precisely why we'd been hired. I'd certainly signed a contract but, not having an agent in those days or any real clue about what I was doing, I'm sure it was a pretty rudimentary document.

Anyway, this Equity man also pointed out that whichever actor was appointed as Equity Deputy would receive an extra shilling in the pound. So I immediately put myself forward for the job, though it was to cause me a lot of trouble.

As Equity Dep I was summoned to a court hearing in order to testify against the producer. I went in clutching my chief piece of evidence, which was my diary. This was, and has remained, not much more than a record of financial transactions. ("Bought a new dress for ten and six. I won't tell Mother!") But it also contained details of all the towns and cities we'd played – together with all the 'week out' entries, and sometimes the 'two weeks out' entries. The producer ended up having to pay a fine.

That producer was Philip Hindin, whom I never met again. Though I did catch sight of him many years later at a Water Rats do, when his table had a banner over it bearing his name, indicating that he'd actually been King Rat at one time. I thought I'd love to go over and say "You may not remember me, but..."

Then again, of course, he might have done!

* * *

After this I noticed an advertisement in *The Stage*, asking for girls aged 18 to 21 for a revue at the Brighton Grand. I knocked a few years off my age and got the job. (This is why reference books still give my date of birth as 1933.) This was also the show when my stage name – Elizabeth J Winch – was changed. The producers didn't like it and gave me a choice of biscuit names to choose from. I refused Crawford, McVitie, McFarlane, even Huntley & Palmer. I settled instead for a more obscure brand – Fraser.

So I was now Elizabeth Fraser. New name, new age!

As it turned out, the revue in Brighton didn't last long and I went straight into a play called *Woman of the Year*. This one was seen in London and was about a sex change – very topical. Yootha Joyce was also in it but the reviews were pretty terrible; in fact, I called it "a real stinker" in my own diary. Kenneth Tynan said that during the course of the play he worked out that the leading actor's name, Rojina Manclark, was an anagram of Major Ian Clark – and that was his entire review!

My next play was called *Hot Water*, written by and starring a marvellous comic actor called Glenn Melvyn. Glenn's previous play, *The Love Match*, had starred Arthur Askey and been a big hit in the West End. This was the sequel, but it didn't get beyond a provincial tour.

I was cast in the part played by Arthur's daughter Anthea in the original play. Also in the company was Ronnie Barker, who I remember had a girlfriend with him.

"Don't mention the word *feet* to her," he warned everyone. "She's very strange about it. Feet terrify her; even the word makes her upset."

I thought this very odd but was careful never to mention feet in her presence. I only realised years later that it was just a very witty leg pull; it was obviously a joke and it took me over 50 years to get it.

The one time Ronnie and I met again, I didn't mention feet but I did mention money. I said to him, "Ronnie, do you remember that play where we were all on £6 a week?"

"Oh!" he said. "I got £8."

I was quite shocked!

* * *

Having toured and toured with various shows it was time for me to share my talents with the BBC. No commercial TV was available as yet, remember.

I became telephone mates with Bush Bailey, who cast the 'extra' roles. You received about £6 for just appearing in a crowd and I'd manage to be in about two a week. A nice little earner. Fred Emney, Vic Oliver, David Nixon, Peter Cushing – they all had me wafting across their sets, carrying trays or having a dance in the background.

And then, my final triumph – I had a line. The scene was one of those auctions held from the back of a van, with lots of suckers crowding round, hoping for a bargain.

"Who will buy this beautiful vase?" the auctioneer shouted at the watching group.

"I will!" I said. "I'll buy it!"

Success at last. If you had lines you received the princely sum of £10. I'd finally hit the jackpot. The world was my oyster. It really was an exciting time for me.

As we now had electricity in our back room, Mother would sit glued to the TV screen and say, "Was that you walking past Peter Cushing, saying 'Excuse me'?"

"Yes, yes!" I'd reply. "That was me!"

She got so used to seeing me she became quite blasé about it. "Your hair doesn't shine very much on television, does it?" Eventually, her only ambition was for me to be in *Crossroads*. To be honest, I resisted that.

I also started to get into films – in a very small way at first. One of my first screen jobs was in 1954, when the advertising firm Pearl & Dean made a promotional film for Butlin's holiday camps. The idea was that Butlin's campers would be "served by happy smiling waitresses," so my happy smiling face was seen on a continual loop in the company's Oxford Street window display. I urged all my friends to get down there and look at me.

There was also an office on St Martin's Lane where Ronnie Curtis cast small parts for B pictures – produced by the Danziger Brothers and such. We would-be's sat in a tiny room and Ronnie would come out of his office, point a finger and say "YOU!"

Trouble was, he was as cross-eyed as dear old Marty Feldman and about three of us would get up. I did get lucky several times but I can't remember saying any lines.

My first proper film part, though, was in an Ealing comedy directed by Michael Truman called *Touch and Go*, with Jack Hawkins and June Thorburn. Alfred Burke was also in it, as 'man on the bridge'. I was 'girl on the bridge'. We had a bit of dialogue and stood on Albert Bridge together for days. The thing I remember most is looking out over the Thames and watching all the discarded condoms going up and down. It was the only thing to look at; in fact, I saw them every day. Tidal, you see.

For some reason, I was billed by my old name, Elizabeth Winch, in this film. The embarrassing thing, though, was how much I was paid. I got £10 a day for ten days. I actually lied to my mother about it because I was so ashamed at being paid so much for doing so little. It seemed ridiculous given how hard she was working for a great deal less.

To save money in those early days, Mother and I had a system which she considered completely immoral. I'd ring her from a telephone box and put in the two pennies. There was a 'press button B' to get your money back if there was no answer and a 'press button A' to lose the cash in order to talk. I asked Mother to quickly say "No message" if there was nothing to report, or "Message" if there was. She hated doing it, thinking it tantamount to theft.

However, one day… Eureka!

"Message."

Press button A.

"The Association of Redundancy want you," she said.

I was signing on at the Labour Exchange at the time; you did that to keep your insurance card stamps up to date. However, once Mother had given the message I realised she'd meant Associated-Rediffusion!

Commercial TV was only just starting up. In fact, the Kingsway office I reported to was more or less empty. The director Tania

Lieven was preparing ITV's very first live show, *The Geranium*, and all she asked me to do was to walk from a mark on the floor to another mark and then stop. I did this three times and got the job. She could see that I could walk naturally without looking for my marks and that was all she wanted. I played a maid (of course), carrying a tray, and had a few lines to speak.

I did another live play for Tania a bit later, *Two Ducks on a Pond*. Another maid, but with more lines. My theatrical experience was paying off.

* * *

Unfortunately, those clever people at Southwark Council decided to pull down a whole block of houses and shops in order to extend Harper Road School. A solicitor was hired by the residents, none of whom had even met a solicitor. But in vain. People were wrenched out of their houses and rehoused in dreadful, giant blocks of flats at the Elephant and Castle. My mother actually wept.

That parcel of land, incidentally, has never been built on to this day. It's just a big walled-off chunk of waste ground. A documentary could be made about this momentous cock-up.

All the shopkeepers were offered alternative shop space elsewhere but the deal was far from appealing. It doesn't sound very much now, but the weekly rental was an outrageous £17-10s. My mother chose to retire from shopkeeping and went with my brother to live in a council house in Dulwich. This gave me the opportunity to fly the nest, so I shared a flat with a couple of girls in Archway.

Philip, incidentally, had worked his way up by this time and was Groceries Manager of the wonderland that was Fortnum & Mason. I'd see him looking resplendent in his tail coat, with a carnation in his buttonhole – every inch the gentleman. Among his best customers were the Docker family. Lord and Lady Docker were fabulously rich and forever in the newspapers. Every Christmas they'd present him with a Fortnum's hamper and we'd tuck in to this luxurious food. I was eating scallops when nobody else knew what a scallop was.

* * *

The BBC had Britain's first ever soap opera, *The Grove Family*, in which I'd made an appearance or two. Naturally, the commercial channel wanted something similar and the result was *Sixpenny Corner*.

I was delighted to be cast in this daily show (which was in many ways a precursor to *Coronation Street*) and got six months' work out of it. Patricia Dainton was the star, the episodes lasted 15 minutes each and the show revolved around an East End garage. My character, Julie Perkins, worked there alongside the owner Bill (Howard Pays) and went out with his brother Stan (Robert Desmond).

I have an old review from a January 1956 copy of the *Daily Mail* in which Peter Black comments on "the extraordinarily bad impersonations of accents by the actors," adding that

> Elizabeth Fraser, as Julie Perkins – and don't ask me who she is because I can't remember – was the only player whose ear was accurately tuned to the idiom of cockney speech. The rest either reproduced the stage music-hall dialect or just didn't bother.

How ironic, since I'd spent years and years trying to iron out my natural cockney. That's what actors did in those days. It wasn't like *EastEnders*!

A couple of months after that we did an episode in which Stan tried his hand as a stage magician, with Julie as his assistant. The act featured a mouse called Myrtle that escaped and ran up Julie's leg while she was trying to sing. John Lemont, the producer, was keen to find a suitable song for me. So one morning, while I was travelling on the tube to the studios at Wembley, I thought up a tune and some lyrics.

It was called 'You Must Be Using Magic On Me' and proved popular in the programme. It was then published by Francis, Day & Hunter, whose offices were opposite Foyles on the Charing Cross Road. I'd become a songwriter over night – though the royalties were a bit slower. "I hear of people who earn a fortune with one song," I told a journalist about 18 months later. "Mine has brought me in £7-5s-10d so far."

I couldn't read music so I'd 'la la la' my tunes to the publishers' pianist and he'd transcribe them. I'd then draft the accompanying lyrics and put the two together. I came up with something like half a dozen songs that way. Among them were 'Alphabet Mambo', 'Lonesome Blues', 'Set 'Em Up, Joe!' and 'Why Didn't You Warn Me?' Unfortunately, the one I liked best, 'Keep All Your Kisses On Ice', never saw the light of day. I'd written it with Eartha Kitt in mind. But, despite the fact that I was friendly at the time with the composer Ronnie Cass (who had access to her 'people'), Eartha never got to see it.

When not writing songs, I was also appearing in several other TV shows. For the BBC, for example, I often popped up in *Dixon of Dock Green*, starring the lovely Jack Warner. I played a Teddy Girl in one. As the shows were performed live, there were green lights to tell you to speed up and red to slow down. A bit like traffic lights really.

They also had a 'cut key', which they'd use if someone forgot their words; the key would cut the sound briefly while the prompter shouted out the missing line. It happened to me one horrible time during an episode of *Dixon of Dock Green*, but I covered up so well that later people said to me, "Ooh, that girl let you down, didn't she? She forgot her lines!" Actually it was me of course, but I didn't let on.

So there you are. Drama School. Panto. Tours and television. A film or two. Even some songwriting. I wasn't doing too badly at all.

CHAPTER THREE

I Married a Thief

Don't let anyone tell you that working with Tony Hancock was a trial. For not only was his comic timing the best I've ever encountered, he was also extremely generous when it came to sharing out the laughs among everyone.

I first worked with Tony in 1956 on his Associated-Rediffusion programme *The Tony Hancock Show*. *Hancock's Half Hour* on BBC Radio was already a big hit and it was Jack Hylton who tempted him into television. The ITV show ran to two series and I was in all the episodes, as far as I remember, alongside familiar Hancock faces like Terence Alexander, Clive Dunn, June Whitfield, Johnny Vyvyan and Dick Emery.

But it was the BBC's television version of *Hancock's Half Hour* that was to make Tony the best-loved comedian in Britain. My first episode, 'The Dancer', involved various Teds – both boys and girls – in a dance hall. Tony observes Sid James' easy way of getting partners – just by nudging their legs and indicating the dance floor – so decides to try the same routine on me. Of course, I kick him back and say, "Who are you kicking, you great lump?"

This seemed like a good start and in fact I returned in the very next episode, 'The Bequest'. This time Tony is looking for a wife and I'm one of the girls supplied by the marriage bureau. The delightful Irene Handl was in that too and insisted, as always, on having her little chihuahua with her – and this was live television! Sid had a little scene to do with Irene and the dog nipped him.

I could see Sid biting his lip and somehow holding back the appropriate expletive. I saw him afterwards and he was muttering, "That bloody dog!" That made Tony laugh a lot.

Anyway, Tony and I had a very funny scene together which ended with Tony uncorking a bottle of champagne. On the night the champagne exploded in my face, though I didn't mind so much because it was quite a good one. Not Dom Perignon, but not bad.

Also around this time, I appeared in several of Benny Hill's shows for the BBC, all done live. One of the things that impressed me most about Benny was his complete absence of ego. He was a big star, probably the first big star created by television. But it never once went to his head. We'd go into a corner café while rehearsing – we worked at Riverside Studios, just as I did for the Hancock shows – and Benny would just have a bread roll and a cup of tea. There was no extravagance about Benny, and we'd always go Dutch – which was fine.

At the end of a series he'd go off abroad somewhere to get away from it all but take virtually no luggage with him. Just a toothbrush. He'd pick up fresh shirts or whatever in the local shops. You couldn't say anything nasty about Benny; he was generous, charming and truly delightful.

As well as the TV shows, I did a month with Benny at the Liverpool Empire. He was on a variety tour and his feed had let him down at the last minute. When he called me up I was more than happy to take over as I understood exactly how he worked and we played off each other really well.

I was very much the straight man. That seemed to be my role in those days and I got to work with pretty much every top comedian in the country. Tommy Cooper, Vic Oliver, Charlie Drake, Eric Sykes, Arthur Askey, Bernard Bresslaw, Peter Sellers, Terry-Thomas, Frankie Howerd, Fred Emney, Terry Scott, Bill Maynard, Harry Secombe, Alan Young, Eric Barker, Jimmy Edwards. The lot.

Eric Sykes was a man I very much admired both as a writer and a performer; he died in 2012 and is much missed. I remember he once asked me to do a live show with him at Olympia in Earls Court. For some reason I was dressed as Britannia and in the middle of our act the stage simply collapsed. It got the biggest laugh of the night.

For my money Tommy Cooper was the funniest man there ever was. I'd actually known him for several years before we worked together on television. We first met in a cinema, where I was watching Alec Guinness in the Ealing comedy *The Man in the White Suit*.

There weren't many people there – it was an afternoon screening – but sitting next to me was a big man who was laughing so much he got the whole audience doing the same. His laughter was so infectious, and of course I joined in too. When the lights came up I recognised him and said, "Oh goodness, it's you!" He suggested we have a salt beef sandwich together so off we went to a favourite little café of his next to the Windmill Theatre.

We became firm friends, and I got to know him even better when my future husband, Bill Hitchcock, directed some of his TV shows in the late 1960s. In fact, Tommy's wife Gwen read my palm once and said I'd end up as an alcoholic. Well, I didn't – though there's still time!

* * *

I had a new boyfriend by this time, name of Michael. He was the son of a well-known character actor and, according to my two flat-mates in Archway, was extremely boring. I didn't think so, but one day we took a walk in the park and I decided to test him by not starting up the conversation myself.

After we'd walked in complete silence for a while, I turned round and told him, "You haven't said one word all this way. You've got no conversation, do you know that?"

"Well," he said, "you always kill the conversation stone dead!"

"Do I?" I replied. I was quite shocked.

We then walked past a pond and he asked, "Do you know the difference between a male duck and a female one?"

Well, that was easy. The male, I said, was always the most colourful one. A few steps further on he observed that many people carried cameras. I agreed at some length. Then a man went by, walking his dog.

"Did you know that a well-trained dog is a happy one?" Michael asked.

"No," I said.

"There you are! That's what I mean," he said. "Always killing the conversation stone dead..."

At that point I decided my flat-mates had been right and never saw him again.

He did have a car, though. Ever since my days as an evacuee I'd had a thing about cars; they were important to me and still are. I'd got used to the luxury of having a boyfriend who drove me around to places, but I didn't have a car of my own. So, after recording the Benny Hill and Tony Hancock shows, I'd generally take a black cab home to my flat in Archway.

One Christmas Eve Tony and I were walking down Kingsway after rehearsals and popped into Verrey's Bar on Regent Street. We proceeded to get extremely drunk and shared a cab home. I was clutching lots of little bottles of sherry that I wanted to keep as a souvenir. There was some kissing and cuddling on the back seat and at one point he put his hand up my skirt. I stopped him and we had a good laugh about it. He didn't come in for coffee, that's for sure.

One of my flat-mates was foolish enough to get pregnant. The other one – who worked at Gerry's, a Shaftesbury Avenue club run by the actor Gerald Campion – suggested we put her in a very hot bath and dose her up with gin. Which is exactly what we did, and as a result she miscarried. These days she could just take a tablet. She eventually took up with a rich man (who had a particularly beautiful car – an Armstrong Siddeley) and married him.

My own love life took a new turn when I went to a friend's 21st birthday party. I met a chap there called Peter Yonwin, whom

I took to immediately; in fact, we made a date there and then. At one point, however, the birthday girl, Margery, came running downstairs in a panic, saying that all her money had been stolen. It was very awkward – there were only about 20 of us there and it was obvious that one of us had taken it, though no one owned up. It was only much later that I realised who the culprit must have been.

That's right. Peter.

When we first met, Peter was acting in Swanage and I'd visit him there as often as I could. I didn't sleep with him though; I just wanted to spend time with him. We dated for a very long time but I had reservations about marrying another actor. I was well aware of the financial insecurities involved and, given that he wasn't getting anywhere near as much work as me, I didn't fancy being the chief breadwinner either.

He was very keen on me, though – or at least very keen to get me into bed – and went so far as to give up acting and take a regular job as a sales rep for Quaker Oats. Not only did this give him a steady income but also a nice new company car – a Mini shooting-brake. Suddenly he became even more attractive than before!

* * *

Having made my first feature film, *Touch and Go*, for Ealing Studios, I went up for the role of the cinema usherette in another Ealing film, *The Smallest Show on Earth*, but Michael Relph and Basil Dearden cast June Cunningham instead. She seemed to fit the bill a lot better than me: platinum blonde hair, big eye-lashes, hour-glass figure. Of course, the part seems perfect for me in retrospect, but in those days I was still quite buttoned-up.

Relph and Dearden must have seen something they liked, though, because I was cast as one of the audience members in the cinema. Keep your eyes peeled and you'll see me during the chaotic screening of the Western.

A bit later I popped up briefly in two other Ealing films – folding sheets in a hotel room with Peter Finch in *The Shiralee* and then playing a waitress in *Davy*, which starred Harry Secombe. In that one I was working for the first time with Joan Sims, whom I admired very much and who was to become a great friend and colleague.

I had a better part in the Herbert Wilcox film *Wonderful Things*, playing the small but showy role of a hot-dog girl. Frankie Vaughan was the male lead and the sweetest of men. I still have a note from Wilcox, dated the 2nd of June 1958, in which he wrote

> I would certainly like to use you again as you did so terribly well in *Wonderful Things*. I am sure you will be glad to know that it had a great reception at the first showing.

Wilcox and his wife Anna Neagle took me under their wing really, and years later I could barely believe it when Dame Anna came round after a show at the Richmond Theatre to compliment me on my performance.

Sadly, nothing really came of *Wonderful Things* – in the short term anyway. For the time being, I was considered a television actress and that was that.

By this time I was appearing on TV all the time and earning a good living. I still didn't have an agent but was being looked after informally by April Young of Kavanagh Productions. I was also well known to big TV names like Albert Stevenson, Bush Bailey, Duncan Wood and Monty Lyon.

One of my most prominent roles came along in late 1957, when I played the School Matron in the Frank Muir and Denis Norden series *Whack-O!* for the BBC. Jimmy Edwards was the star and was always a laugh both off the set and on. The shows were all put out live from the Shepherd's Bush Empire, and Jimmy would frequently forget his lines. I'd start filling in with my next line only for Jimmy, as the Headmaster, to suddenly hold up his hand and cry "Back,

Matron, back!" – he'd just remembered the forgotten line and wanted to get it in after all.

It was a very happy show but, impossible as it may seem these days, poor Arthur Howard (who was Leslie Howard's brother and played the assistant headmaster) was outed as a homosexual and dropped. This was particularly outrageous since Jimmy was gay too.

Whack-O! brought me some of my earliest fan letters. Most were quite straightforward, like this one from Newport in South Wales.

> Dear Madame
> Please will you send me an autographed photograph of yourself.
>
> Your performance as 'Matron' is so good that you might almost be a *real* Matron. Hoping you will oblige.
>
> Best wishes and good luck ... etc

Others were concerned that my role should be given more of a boost. This one was actually addressed to the writers and forwarded to me by Kavanagh Productions.

> Dear Messrs Muir & Norden
> As a pensioner I enjoy the antics of the school-boys in *Whack-O!* and Jimmy Edwards as the Headmaster.
>
> But I do think you could write the piece to let us see more of the Matron – she did show her nice legs once and should do it again.
>
> I hope it's all right for me to write to you.
> Best wishes ... etc

A writer from Gillingham made a similar point on 23 October.

> Dear Miss Fraser
> Please forgive me for writing to you, but I do so as a keen follower of the *Whack-O!* series.

> Two weeks ago I had the temerity to write to the producer, to 'complain' of the scant opportunities given to the Matron. In the first programme your appearance was fleeting, and your absence conspicuous in the second.
>
> I further commented that your uniform was (shall we say) too 'matronly'.
>
> Mr [Douglas] Moodie was gracious enough to acknowledge my carping criticism, but I do not suppose he lost much sleep or rushed into any re-planning of your part.
>
> Anyway, last evening my criticism was assuredly thrown right back in my lap, for you were allowed to spread your wings a little at last. I am now indulging in a quite smug 'I told you so' feeling, as having anticipated a 'winner'.
>
> So, to place the credit where it is due, I would like to thank *you* for having brought some engaging and necessary glamour to what was in danger of becoming a purely schoolboyish romp.
>
> May I then wish you happiness in future programmes of the series, and all success in anything else you undertake.
>
> Yours sincerely ... etc

Other letters weren't quite so encouraging. This one from East London was written a year later; in fact, it's dated 31 October 1958.

> I saw you in *Murder Bag* the other evening and I certainly look forward to more frequent appearances in the future. I could be wrong, of course, but I do really think that you have everything it takes to achieve at least moderate

> success, and you can believe me when I tell you I am not easily pleased.

Nice to know he thought I'd be at least 'moderately' successful!

* * *

One TV job I really enjoyed wasn't so much a show as an extended advert. It was an episode of *Jim's Inn* and starred Jimmy Hanley. People would call it blatant product placement nowadays but the advertising had to be slipped across in the context of a proper programme. Jimmy played a pub landlord who'd sell someone a packet of cigarettes, say, and rather than carefully conceal the brand would keep it in shot and actually have a detailed conversation with the customer about what a good brand it was.

The funniest experience I had with that kind of advertising programme – ad-mags, they were called – was for Ian Fordyce at Associated-Rediffusion. This one went out live. I'd been signed up for the Star House Tin Foil section of the show, but when the current Miss England couldn't read the narration properly for the Janet Dickinson Swimwear section I was hastily roped into doing that as well. As for the tin foil, I was accompanied by another girl who shall remain nameless for the very good reason that I never found out her name.

We were two girls sitting on a studio beach with a picnic hamper. She was meant to bring out various food items she'd wrapped and I was to say, "Ooh, what's that?"

"Why," she'd say, "this is Star House Tin Foil."

Tin foil for food was a completely new idea at the time, so my character quite naturally replied, "Oh really? What's it used for then?"

I was clearly the feed, giving her the opportunity to explain how you could cook with tin foil as well as just wrap things in it. "Gosh, that's wonderful," I'd say at the end of this explanation. "How much is it?"

"Well, it's one and eleven for the small size and two and eleven for the large."

"Ooh, I'll get some then," I'd say, and that was it.

All this went smoothly in rehearsal but when the live transmission began this other girl completely dried. The sandwiches came out but then she just froze.

"Ooh," I said, "what's that?" Nothing. "Erm," I improvised, "is that the stuff I've been reading about?" Nothing. "Erm ... That's Star House Tin Foil, isn't it?" Silence again. "I suppose you can use it for anything, can't you?" Still nothing.

I began to quite enjoy myself at this point. "Well, it's obvious you can use it for wrapping sandwiches. But I've heard you can cook with it too. You can cook meat with it – it really brings the flavour out. That's wonderful, isn't it?" Silence. "Well, I think so anyway."

I then took a deep breath, slapped my thigh and finished up with: "Now, I expect you're going to ask me how much it is. Well, it's one and eleven for the small size and two and eleven for the large."

I'd somehow got us through it and afterwards Ian Fordyce came down and kissed me. "You were marvellous!" he said. "We were dying up there in the control box. But you were absolutely fantastic. I shall use you till the end of my days!"

It's one of my happiest memories of working in television. Though not, I expect, for the other girl. She was never seen again.

* * *

I liked Peter Yonwin a lot but didn't really love him. In fact, I think the only reason he stuck around so long was because I kept refusing him sex. When I was growing up, it simply wasn't done to have sex before marriage. I remembered a customer of my mother's, known as Riggy, who'd become pregnant out of wedlock and was talked about in hushed tones by the entire street. So I was determined to be a virgin on my wedding night.

One Thursday afternoon Peter and I were out for a drive when he suddenly stopped the car outside Wood Green Registry Office. He said if we didn't go in and set a date for the wedding he'd never see me again. So we went in and registered for the 22nd of November 1958. That was about a month away, so I thought I'd have time to think things through and cancel if necessary. But, to my horror, when we got back to his mother's place he promptly phoned *my* mother and announced that we were getting married! My brother immediately organised the catering (Fortnum & Mason, of course) and my mother bought a hat.

So that was that. We got married. As for the much anticipated wedding night, quite frankly I can't remember anything about it. Whether it was good, bad or indifferent I really don't know.

I quickly found out what kind of man Peter really was. His mother had kept him for years and even gone into debt for him. Now it looked as if it was going to be my turn. Unknown to me at the time, he'd been accused of stealing the 'tronk' at Quaker Oats and had been given the sack – even before our wedding. The tronk was the expenses fund for the firm's travelling salesmen; it was never proved that he'd taken the money but it's more than likely he did. Anyway, he was determined to keep me so he soon got another job as a sales rep for Thomas Hedley Ltd, selling Camay and other soap products.

Peter's mother let us have the top part of her house in Wood Green as a flat and within a day or two of moving in my piggy bank was smashed and all the money taken. Being utterly naïve, I thought it might have been his mother's cleaner – and Peter did nothing to dissuade me.

Straight afterwards he announced that we were going off for our honeymoon to Windsor. It was an expensive hotel and, when I wondered if we could afford it, Peter assured me he could. Well, of course he could – it was *my* money! Like the mystery over Margery's 21st birthday party, I only found out the truth about all this much later.

Another time he came home with a huge box containing 144 back brushes. They had the Camay brand on them and he claimed that they were surplus stock. In fact, they were meant to be distributed to customers as free gifts and he'd just decided to take them. For years afterwards everyone who knocked at my door was surprised to be given a back brush.

One day when Peter wasn't feeling well he asked me to phone work and tell them he couldn't come in. The receptionist told me that two of the bosses would be coming over to see him, and – naïve as ever – I thought how sweet it was of them to drop in personally and see how he was. When they arrived, however, they sat us both down and asked me if I realised that Peter hadn't been into work for six weeks.

Apparently they'd put a detective onto him. Little did I know that, on leaving for work in the mornings, Peter had been going to Manor House, having his breakfast, buying a paper and then sitting on a bench to read it. Then he was off to the bookmakers and finally the greyhound track.

I said, "But he's working on his orders every night!"

"Yes," they replied, "but he's just been making them up."

People who wanted to place orders had never seen a rep while other customers were having stuff delivered that they hadn't ordered. I remembered him saying on many occasions that he couldn't come out for a drink in the evening because he had too much work to do. And, worst of all, he'd blamed me when they first queried his absences. His wife was an actress, he'd said, and made him go out all the time. When in reality I'd been sitting at home watching him fill out these non-existent orders.

Peter listened to all this in complete silence. When the men said they were going to prosecute him, I begged them not to. My career was just taking off and – in those days, anyway – it would have been bad publicity. From then on, however, I knew that my husband was living in a fantasy world.

CHAPTER FOUR

Who is Cynthia?

By the time I married Peter I was still without an agent but was doing very well on television. I was playing everything from a cave-girl in *The Benny Hill Show* to a cat burglar in *Dixon of Dock Green.*

But what about films?

Well, whenever the call went out for a young comedy actress, I was turned down on a depressingly regular basis. At that time, if you were Joan Sims or Dora Bryan you were working in films pretty much all the time. If neither was available, producers would employ somebody else. Unfortunately, I didn't really fit the Joan or Dora mould. Nor was I a Marilyn Monroe or Anita Ekberg type. Looking back, I suppose I wasn't making the most of myself. I'd had a lovely set of photos done by a photographer friend, Eddie Brind, but they certainly weren't glamour shots. They were more Kay Kendall than Diana Dors.

Sonny Zahl had an office in the April Young Agency, and I remember him saying to me, "Look, there's nothing available for women. It's all films about men and war. Just take a look at this new script that's come in this morning. *I'm All Right Jack* it's called. There's only one girl in it!"

"Only one girl in it?" I thought. "Oh well..."

That 'one girl', it turned out, was Cynthia Kite. The Boulting Brothers, John and Roy, were trying to cast the role and word had got round that they were having no luck. So every agent in town was putting girls forward. Finally Richard Attenborough said to John, "Look, you've tried everybody. Why not look in *Spotlight*? There might be somebody in there who hasn't *got* an agent."

Apparently Richard went ahead and phoned Kenneth Seale, who was still the editor of *Spotlight* and remembered me from my drama school days – back when he'd told me that Weston Drury was wrong and that I *could* play comedy. He'd followed my career ever since and now just phoned me direct and told me to get down to Shepperton.

When I got there John Boulting took one look at me and said, in his delightfully plummy voice, "I'm very sorry but you're just not right for the part."

"But I've appeared in hundreds of TV shows," I protested.

"Well," he replied, "that's nothing to be proud of, my dear!" To him and plenty of others, television really was the lowest of the low.

"I've come by two buses and a train to get here," I persisted. "And I've walked to the studio. *And* I've learned the part."

So he relented and sent me into Make-Up, saying we'd do the audition after lunch.

That 60-minute lunch break was probably the most important hour of my career. The people at Shepperton put a long blonde wig on me, applied long eye-lashes, got rid of my buttoned-up cardigan and squeezed me into a very tight sweater with a very tight belt. I'd managed to conceal the fact that I was a 37-24-37 double D for so long but now it seemed like an asset.

This different me went on set and John was immediately impressed. He'd been so convinced I was wrong for the part that he'd sent Ian Carmichael home. Ian was recreating his Stanley Windrush role from the Boultings' film *Private's Progress* and he'd played in the tests for all the other potential Cynthia Kites. The famous bubble car sequence was the chosen scene. But now I was sitting in the bubble car with the studio manager, Philip Shipway.

I smothered him with kisses and relaxed back onto his lap on the line, "Are them your own teeth?" It was a real gift to me, that line, and it's still my favourite line in the film.

Also, my expert knowledge of cricket came in handy. Both John and Roy were mad about cricket and none of the other candidates had known anything about it. Even so, there was no fanfare. No big moment. I just went home to my lying husband and assumed I wouldn't get the part.

Then a couple of days later Philip Shipway called with the news that I had! So I got back in touch with Sonny Zahl and he negotiated a deal for me of £50 a week plus a car to take me to and from the studio. It was a lovely car, too. It was a very bleak winter at the beginning of 1959 and the car would come through the fog each morning to pick me up at Wood Green.

* * *

John Boulting was directing the film and I thought he was wonderful. I had to stay at his house on several occasions owing to the thick fog, and I realised then how happily married he was! He did play a part, however, in changing my name in a different way.

On the very first day, I arrived at the studio to find my name printed on the back of a chair. Hang on, though… Who? Liz Fraser? They'd shortened my name. Actually, John had mentioned this to me already. Being called Elizabeth Fraser on British TV was fine, but films were international and there was a well-known American actress of the same name (Elisabeth Fraser). She played Sgt Bilko's on-off girlfriend in *The Phil Silvers Show*.

So my name had to be changed. Nothing radical. John suggested Liz Fraser. I liked it. I liked it a lot. I went ahead and registered my new name with Equity and was, as far as I know, the first 'Liz' ever listed in *Spotlight*.

The other chairs at Shepperton had some pretty impressive names on them. Television may have been considered low-class by filmmakers but most of the actors on the film had been on TV at some time or other. In fact, I'd worked with nearly all of them except Margaret Rutherford. I was a big fan of hers and playing opposite her was an extraordinary experience. It was a privilege just to meet her.

One of the lovely things about her was the fact that she made certain her husband was given a part in every film she did. Stringer Davis was a charming old boy and later on would be given the important supporting role of Mr Stringer in all the Miss Marple films Margaret did. In *I'm All Right Jack*, however, he was just one of the many journalists who besiege Fred Kite's house after he's called a strike.

I remember Margaret saying on the set, "Well, he's got to have a few lines."

So he did.

Irene Handl, who played my mother, was another favourite. In real life she was full of malapropisms, so when directing her John would start out by letting her do every malapropism in the book.

Then he'd say, "Let's just do one take straight."

And, of course, that was the take they'd use. I'd work with Irene many times over the years and became very fond of her.

The person the press and public *really* went mad for on *I'm All Right Jack* was Peter Sellers. Although I was only five years his junior, I was playing Peter's daughter. I'd first met him during my earliest days on television. In fact, we were doing a sketch in which Peter, Irene and me were in an orchestra pit; it was probably for *The Dickie Valentine Show*. We all knew one another in those days. He lived round the corner from me at the time and from the very first day we met he was trying it on. And he never stopped trying for the next several years.

He was a very acquisitive person, always wanting to have the latest thing. His major passions were cars and cameras, plus women of course. But if he could choose between them, I think he'd have gone for cameras. He was always showing me the latest models, and on one occasion he asked me to pose for him. Not only that – he wanted to do some topless shots. "Certainly not!" I said.

I met his wife Anne as we went up to Peter's studio at the top of the house, and the pictures he took remain among my favourites of all the photos I've ever had taken. They certainly weren't the pictures he'd wanted to take, however, because everything he did was aimed at getting one into bed.

One person he succeeded with was a close friend of mine called June. Peter had made *The Mouse That Roared* directly before *I'm All Right Jack* and somehow June had become his secretary. She loved him very much but he was married and so was she. He quickly started taking her for granted, as he did with all the women he had affairs with.

He had his own personal manager by then, as well as his agent. This man was called Bill, worked from offices round the back of Leicester Square and managed Peter's affairs in more ways than one. Peter would call Bill at lunch times and tell him to send June over to the MGM studios at Elstree. Peter said he needed her for 'dictation' purposes but in fact he wanted sex for lunch. She'd turn up, he'd satisfy himself and then send her back to London. He'd then have a light snack and be ready for the afternoon's shooting.

This had been going on for months and June said she was beginning to feel like a prostitute. So one day she turned up for 'lunch' at MGM and said "No" to him. When she got back to the office she found that all her belongings were already packed up in a box.

Bill said, "I don't know what you've done to upset Peter but he phoned through and told me to dispense with your services."

And that was that.

I was a bit unsure of myself while working on *I'm All Right Jack* so I didn't confront Peter about how he'd treated June until we were making *Two Way Stretch* a few months later. He was completely unapologetic, saying they were both married and both consenting adults. The relationship was pretty meaningless to him so he turned the conversation to cars and cameras instead.

While making *I'm All Right Jack* he'd shown me his latest car, which was pretty miraculous for 1959 because it had automatic windows. That car didn't last very long, though. Nothing did with Peter. He was very fond of his mother and had two very close actor friends, David Lodge and Graham Stark. If there was a female equivalent I suppose it was me, though he did overstep the mark a few times. Peter being Peter, you just forgave him.

He was very focused while playing Fred Kite but the character certainly didn't take him over. I enjoyed our scenes together and also enjoyed watching the scenes between Peter and Terry-Thomas. Peter and Terry respected each other very much but there was an interesting tension when they acted together because they were so different in technique. Terry tended to be fantastic on the first take and then got steadily worse, whereas Peter would get better and better each time. But they were both determined to get it right so some of their scenes took an awfully long time. The scene with Terry darning Peter's socks, for example, went on and on. It was fascinating to watch.

* * *

I'm All Right Jack is now considered a classic but of course you don't realise you're in a classic while you're making it. A film only becomes classic over time. I was just happy to have been cast. The film was seven weeks of good laughs and hard work. So, on £50 a week, I made the not unattractive sum of £350. Sonny Zahl, of course, got ten per cent of that. Sadly, he committed suicide several years later by throwing himself out of David Frost's office window. What that says about David Frost I'm not sure!

The Boultings advised me against signing up full-time with Sonny and suggested I go for John Redway instead; he was one of the top agents in the country and also represented Peter Sellers. So I signed with John Redway Ltd on the 20th of May 1959.

The Boultings and British Lion had been pushing to sign me up to a seven-year contract even before *I'm All Right Jack* was released. No sooner had I signed with John than they asked me to sign the long-term contract again. My new agent advised me against it, which was ironic since it was John Boulting who'd suggested him in the first place.

Had I signed, I'd have been on £100 a week the following year, with a salary for the seventh year that seemed huge in 1959. But 1966 was a long way off. Had I signed, I would also have been the Boulting Brothers' first ever contract artist. But it would have been the wrong move for me.

Despite not signing with British Lion, I was billed in publicity as "the girl the Boultings picked." I was given a big push – I even appeared on the sheet music for the rock'n'roll number used over the credits – and *I'm All Right Jack* turned out to be a big commercial and critical success.

I found myself doing promotional events alongside several of the fork-lift trucks supplied for the film by Lansing Bagnall, and as a result they offered me a brand-new Ford Anglia fresh off the production line. It wasn't free but they sold it to me at a major discount. It was my first car and I loved it.

I'd already learned to drive, having seen all those lists of useful skills an actor should have, like mastering accents, riding horses and, yes, driving cars. I'd spotted a motoring school opposite the Garrick Theatre and booked in for an initial two-hour session. What I hadn't realised was that if your first lesson is around Trafalgar Square and Hyde Park Corner it's a lot trickier than taking it in, say, Hertfordshire. My teacher was an ex-bus driver and, having driven us to Victoria, he got out of the driver's seat and instructed me to drive back. With buses coming at us from every angle I was scared out of my wits.

But I had a few more lessons later on, during which, being a bus driver, he taught me how to double de-clutch. I then passed my test first time and found that I'd become a very good and fearless driver. Friends who learned in the countryside refuse to drive in London.

* * *

Thanks to the Boulting Brothers, I now found myself with a new image – and film offers came pouring in. In fact, I had several films lined up even during production on *I'm All Right Jack*. So pleased was John Boulting with his new 'discovery' that he had already alerted other film producers to his great find. Among others he phoned Basil Dearden and Michael Relph, who cast me in *Desert Mice*.

This was a lovely film with lovely people – Sid James, Irene Handl, Dora Bryan, Alfred Marks, Dick Bentley. It was all about the old wartime ENSA tours and gave me a chance to meet Basil and Michael again after my tiny bit in *The Smallest Show on Earth* two years before.

When I reminded them of this, Basil said, "Really? Oh, you would've been so good as the usherette. Why on earth didn't your agent put you up for that part?"

"Well," I replied, "you saw me for it but didn't cast me!"

I'd worked with most of the *Desert Mice* cast many times on television and we had a great time together. We'd gone over-schedule, however, so one Friday Basil decided to work overtime in order to complete the film. He checked this with the technicians but didn't consult the actors. Sid pointed out that we should do something about this and Irene suggested we appoint an Equity Deputy.

So all these experienced film and TV people elected the most inexperienced of the lot – Dick Bentley. He was a big smash on radio in *Take It From Here* but this was his first film. He was the gentlest of people and all these seasoned actors picked him! So off he went to have a word with Basil Dearden.

Well, he came back as white as a sheet. Basil had apparently told him to "Fuck off!" and said that he'd never use any of us again. We all had plenty of work lined up so we said "Stuff him."

All except poor Reginald Beckwith. He was like a lucky mascot in Basil's films and for years had cropped up in pretty much all of them. I worked with Reginald again a few years later. "You know," he told me, "Basil never did use me again after that."

* * *

By the time *I'm All Right Jack* came out I'd made not only *Desert Mice* but also *The Night We Dropped a Clanger*. People like William Hartnell, Cecil Parker and Leslie Phillips were in it but sadly I didn't have much to do with them. Brian Rix and Leo Franklyn were the leads and I joined them for several personal appearances to promote the film.

I had a little song in there called 'I Want a Man'. Everything had seemed to go fine on the take but when I saw the film it was clear it hadn't. This deep contralto voice came out singing "I want a man who's as tall as a tree..." Obviously they hadn't thought much of my singing voice and had dubbed me. It's quite funny to watch now.

When the film came out, F Leslie Withers of the *Sunday Mercury* pointed out that

> The well-shaped Liz's wardrobe is so scanty in this film she scarcely has a clanger to drop ... The *Clanger* film won't enhance her reputation, but I hope there will be many producers who will remember her true-to-life performance in the Boulting picture. Whether she wants to break away from comedy – or even can – remains to be seen. All I ask is that she isn't forgotten as film-makers tear off across Europe looking for some sex-kitten to play the next cockney role.

That was fair enough. Ever since Brigitte Bardot had come over to star in our very own *Doctor at Sea*, loads of French and Italian sexpots were finding their way into British films. I knew this only too well because my Matron role in *Bottoms Up* – the film version of the *Whack-O!* TV series – was taken by a shapely French woman called Vanda Hudson.

Incidentally, the year after making *The Night We Dropped a Clanger* I appeared in a kind of follow-up called *The Night We Got the Bird*. This time, true to form, I spent most of the film in a nightie. I played Dora Bryan's sister in that. I'd seen Dora in all her West End revues and was a big admirer of hers. In fact, in interviews of the period I claimed that in a few years' time I'd be ready to take on Dora Bryan parts, then a few years after that Kathleen Harrison parts and eventually Margaret Rutherford parts. Wishful thinking!

Rounding off 1959, in October I was reunited with Peter Sellers, at Shepperton again, for *Two Way Stretch*, which we made under the title *Nothing Barred*. It was a prison comedy and in it Peter proved his versatility by playing, not my father, but my boyfriend.

There's a visiting time scene in that film where all the inmates' loved ones smuggle goodies to them through the bars. It was my job to distract the prison warders at the crucial moment by pretending my garter belt had snapped. For my money, the funniest part of the scene was a little exchange between big Arthur Mullard and his little wife, played by Vivienne Martin. She's carrying a baby and Arthur asks, "How old is he now, my love?" She answers, "Eight months, dearest!" "But I've been in here nearly two years," he says. "Oh yes Fred," she replies, "but you've sent me some lovely letters."

Anyway, Peter was very unhappy just before this scene was shot because he'd decided – a good week into filming – that he'd chosen the wrong part. Rather than Dodger Lane, he wanted to play Wilfrid Hyde-White's part, Soapy Stevens. The producers weren't having it, of course, and Peter was very sulky and upset. He told me he was going "to throw the part away" and muttered his way through the visiting time scene. Yet to this day, when people talk about Peter's marvellous film acting, they often show that very scene. He couldn't help being brilliant even when he tried not to be.

On top of everything else, Peter had pneumonia for most of the shoot. Our passionate kissing scenes took take after take to get right – hours, in fact. But this wasn't a ruse on Peter's part; he really wasn't well. Even so, he was still making a play for me throughout the filming. Every day, without fail, he'd suggest we have lunch together in his dressing room. Thanks to June, of course, I knew what lunchtime with Peter involved so I kept well away.

When the film came out, there was a lovely review in *Picturegoer* that said

> There hasn't been such a good laugh about comic crooks since *The Lavender Hill Mob* ... The acting is a director's dream. No need to mention that Sellers is perfect, but it's a tribute to the consummate team-work of all concerned that no one hogs the picture. A special word, though, for Bernard Cribbins and Liz Fraser (Sellers' undulating girlfriend). They are two young artists with a real veteran's sense of comedy and timing.

I seemed to have cornered the market – at last.

It delighted me, in a funny sort of way, when a friend of mine phoned to say she'd gone up for a film part and been turned down because the producer was "looking for a Liz Fraser type." Of course, before the Boulting Brothers came along, I'd been rejected often enough myself for not being that 'type'. But now I was it and felt that if I stuck to that type I wouldn't be out of work for long.

And I was right.

In fact, on New Year's Eve a piece appeared in the *Daily Herald* in which Anthony Carthew pointed out that

> Every year thousands of girls wander hopefully into film studios, looking for a break into stardom. Most of them

> are shown the door. A few live on to decorate premieres. Fewer still get tiny parts. One of those girls made the grade in 1959. Her name is Liz Fraser. After going through the tiny parts routine, she won the coveted part of Peter Sellers' daughter in *I'm All Right Jack*. Now film work is flooding in ... Liz, ex-typist, ex-repertory actress, is to be the Dumb Blonde of 1960.

And *he* was right, too.

CHAPTER FIVE

Up, Up and Away

Just as the *Daily Herald* had predicted, 1960 was a big year for me. The year began with an interesting 'full circle' sort of experience. Having appeared in Associated-Rediffusion's very first live drama, I was now engaged for the very last. It was called *Incident* and was directed by Cyril Coke.

In it, I was playing Alan Bates' wife. It was grim stuff, really. We're living on a council estate and he's so disillusioned with the world he doesn't want our child to grow up in it. So, with me out for the evening, he threatens to throw the baby off the balcony. Eddie Byrne was playing the police inspector desperately trying to track me down. He finds me in the pub – leopard skin coat, heavy make-up, voice soaked in gin and tonic – and tells me what my husband is proposing to do.

"He won't do that," I slurred. "He's never going to do that. He doesn't do anything!"

Anyway, the inspector finally persuades me and drags me back to the estate. Sure enough, there's Alan shouting, "It's the end of the world. I'm going to throw this baby over the edge. It's not a fit world for it to live in."

All this ranting and raving is going on and I'm still not concerned. So the inspector then has a crucial speech in which he convinces me that my husband is serious after all. Only Eddie Byrne forgot to say it!

Bear in mind, of course, that this is live. The speech that bridged the gap for me between drunken apathy and blind panic simply wasn't there. I had to go straight from "Oh no, he won't do that! He's full of hot air" to "No, no! My darling! Our baby! I love you!" without a break. So that was a good one to end on!

It was reassuringly typical of Rediffusion, to be honest.

* * *

'This dumb belle keeps you in fits' was the title of a piece that appeared in *Picturegoer* in April 1960.

> Liz Fraser, the screen's sexiest dumb blonde with the pin-up looks, is making everyone sit up. As the busiest and bounciest blonde stooge in the business, she has the screen comics queuing up for her support.

I certainly was busy that year. Producer Betty Box cast me in the latest Doctor film, *Doctor in Love*, number four in the popular series. Again, I was surrounded by plenty of familiar faces – Joan Sims, Irene Handl, Leslie Phillips, Michael Craig. In fact, Joan and I had to perform a striptease in front of James Robertson Justice. We took it very seriously; striptease is a real skill but the joke was we were meant to be pretty crummy. As for James, he was a very warm, smiling sort of character, completely different from the fierce characters he played on film.

I was also cast by Frank Launder and Sidney Gilliat in *The Pure Hell of St Trinian's*. Sadly I was too old to play an over-developed schoolgirl but I had a nice sexy part as a WPC opposite the delightful Joyce Grenfell and Lloyd Lamble. This was a buttoned-up role, but the jacket was extremely tight. Forty-odd years later, incidentally, I was invited to the premiere of the new *St Trinian's* film; it was nice to be remembered as an 'old girl'.

Joyce Grenfell, whom I'd act with again in *The Americanization of Emily*, was someone I very much admired already. To me, she was like a female Alastair Sim. The way she created a whole audience of schoolchildren in her famous monologues – and made you feel as if they were really there – was extraordinary. She was one of our cleverest comic actresses; her equivalent today would probably be Victoria Wood, whom I also admire.

I also acted with Norman Wisdom in *The Bulldog Breed*. We'd worked together before and it was nice to be reunited with him at Beaconsfield Studios. Our scenes together were very funny and sweet, though I still managed to lose my skirt at one point, which was proving to be the norm by this time. I also got to act opposite a bulldog.

* * *

By the middle of 1960 I'd developed an image as the funny blonde who wore as little clothing as possible. It didn't bother me too much at that point – after all, it was lovely to finish one film and start immediately on another. But when a melodramatic costume romp called *Fury at Smugglers' Bay* was offered to me I felt it would make a refreshing change.

I was cast as a Cornish barmaid who doubles as a highwayman's spy. The rest of the cast made the film even more appealing. I'd met the two juvenile leads, June Thorburn and John Fraser, on my first film, *Touch and Go*. William Franklyn was the dashing highwayman. And the star was that wonderful gentleman, Peter Cushing.

We were filming in Wales, and when we got to the location the director, John Gilling, took me aside and said, "I've been thinking..."

That's always a warning sign.

"You realise we're supposed to be in Cornwall for this film?" he went on.

"Yes..." I replied cautiously.

"Well," said John, "Peter obviously isn't going to play his part with a Cornish accent. He's the Squire. June and John are his children so they wouldn't speak Cornish either. They're both very well spoken. Bill Franklyn doesn't speak Cornish. So there's only one person left who could possibly be Cornish and that's you."

"But I can't do a Cornish accent," I protested.

"Yes, of course you can. You're an actress!"

"I've never done Cornish!" I persisted.

He fixed me with a steely glare and said, "Well, you're doing Cornish now!"

And that was that. I subsequently saw the film in a cinema with a friend of mine – we both paid, it wasn't a preview or anything like that – and I cringed when I came on the screen. My first line, spoken in a very thick and highly unconvincing Cornish accent, was "'Ere's yer soup, zir!" Well, I laughed out loud at this terrible line. But then someone poked me in the back from the seat behind.

"Excuse me," he complained, "we're enjoying this film and we think she's very good!"

Actually, *Fury at Smugglers' Bay* was great fun to make and, after so much comedy, it was nice to have an opportunity to die on screen for the first time. (I've had seven deaths in all.) I was very disappointed, however, because my big death scene was cut from the finished film. I vividly recall shooting it though, because I had a wonderful moment with Bill Franklyn. I'd been shot and he was leaning over me to hear my final words.

"What's your name?" I gasped in my very best Cornish accent.

He was a man of mystery, you see, and I wanted to know his name before I died. I think that would have been one of the great last lines in film history. But, alas, it was cut, never to be seen by anyone.

Undoubtedly my favourite person in the film was Bernard Lee, who a couple of years later was cast as 'M' in the James Bond films. He was a larger than life sort of person and dominated every scene in which he appeared. He and I had to wait for something like two weeks before John Gilling got to our scenes and we therefore spent a lot of time together.

I liked him very much, but he was an alcoholic. He drank and drank and drank, so I tried to get him off the sauce. An impossible task, you might think, but somehow I managed it. We'd go out for a walk in the Welsh countryside and Bernard would spot a lovely rustic pub and make an immediate bee-line for it. I'd say, "No, we're not going into the pub..." And he'd stop in his tracks.

I managed to keep Bernard dry for that entire fortnight. Then on our very first day of shooting he got on his horse and immediately fell off. He picked himself up and came over to me. "If you hadn't stopped me drinking," he said, "I'd have been drunk by now and I wouldn't have fallen off that bloody horse!"

He was very funny and we became great chums.

The sad thing about films, though, is that those friendships can be so transient. You're together for a short time, you make friends, you do the work, and then you never see each other again.

In honour of that escapade with Bernard, I wrote a little poem about him while out on location.

This is the tale of Bernard Lee
Who vomited at the thought of tea
He much preferred a stronger brew –
Champagne, Scotch, plus a gin or two

There came a time when John Redway said
"Now here's a film with damn good pay
But I'm afraid you'll have to go away
And I ought to add, by the way,
That the First Assistant is Phil Shipway"

Now Bernard Lee's bottle-bank was rather low
So he accepted the film and to Wales did go
He arrived at a guest house called Glynymel
Went fishing for trout but didn't do well

Now things went fine until a notification
Was sent by the local population
Enquiring as to Bernard Lee's duration
And signed "in anticipation and trepidation
On behalf of the whole Welsh nation"

They explained that the whole town's pubs now were dry
And those also of the towns nearby
Even Swansea and Cardiff were running low
So they insisted that Mr Lee should go

So Bernard Lee had to sign the pledge
And drank water with his beef and veg
His evenings would see him quietly at play
Sipping coffee with his pal Phil Shipway

The moral of this story is plain to see
When next you drink think of Bernard Lee
For if he hadn't retired, by the by,
I'm afraid all the bloody pubs would now be dry!

My poetry, I'm glad to say, has improved considerably since that time!

* * *

It was also in 1960 that I received a BAFTA nomination as 'Most Promising Newcomer of 1959'. The other nominee was little Hayley Mills, who'd won hearts with her performance in *Tiger Bay*. Hayley got the award but it was an honour just to be nominated. I had my first proper evening gown for the occasion, which the Boulting Brothers had had made for me since I was representing *I'm All Right Jack*. In the end, Hayley beat me twice. She not only won Best Newcomer but also, later on, got her very own Boulting brother – though she married Roy, not John.

Ironically, just as my film career was on the up, my marriage was crashing down. After I'd discovered that Peter was a liar and a thief, he'd started drinking more and more and on one occasion lashed out, perforating my eardrum. To be fair to him, it was a one-off. He didn't normally behave like that. It was a nasty combination of alcohol and his increasing instability.

Peter's former employers at Thomas Hedley Ltd had only agreed not to prosecute if I sent him to a psychiatrist. So we both went to see a specialist at Colney Hatch, and I was told Peter needed help and that twice-weekly sessions would be arranged for him. Tuesdays and Thursdays were the appointed days.

I'd visit Peter at his mother's house once a week. We'd all three sit there with our cups of tea, the log fire burning, and Peter would regale us with tales of the treatment he was being given at the hospital. He told us all about the various strange characters he'd met there, and we became quite used to hearing about all his new friends – Joe the little bald one, Annie with the hats, and so on.

After a while I went to visit my GP. I was understandably depressed. He told me he was going to be completely unethical and show me a letter he'd recently received from the psychiatrist at the hospital. It stated that Peter had never turned up for any of his appointments. Also, in the psychiatrist's expert opinion, Peter was a psychopath and would eventually land up in prison. So I filed for divorce.

Peter later remarried. He was thrown out and was eventually divorced a second time. He then drove a community bus for a while. He died, his second wife told me, in 2008.

* * *

When my divorce from Peter went through I'd recently bought one of four bungalows that were being built in East Barnet. I had little collateral but the Westminster Bank in Piccadilly lent me £5,250 to which I added my savings of £500. It took every penny I had but I was earning good money for my film roles and was able to keep up the payments on my own. Peter, of course, was never to live there with me. In fact, when the divorce came through, I threw an almighty 'I'm Free' party at the bungalow.

There were 82 guests in all and the place rang with laughter. Tommy Cooper came. Sid James. Eric Sykes. Spike Milligan. Charlie Drake. Even Tony Hancock, which surprised everyone because Tony was never one for a party. He was something of a recluse even then but was great company. I'd wanted it to be an amazing party and it turned out to be just that.

Bungalows are great for parties. The hall was converted into a bar and, thanks to my brother's connections at Fortnum & Mason, the catering was of top quality. Everyone was given a raffle ticket on arrival and a bunch of flowers when they left. In one room I'd installed a clairvoyant, with people queuing up for palm readings. And in another I'd set up a roulette table, with Davy Kaye as croupier. The chips were just butter beans but all the wealthy stars there took the game very seriously indeed. In fact, it turned into a bit of a riot. Sid James won the top prize, which was a very good bottle of champagne.

Everyone seemed to know about the party for miles around. In fact, Benny Hill got lost en route and was stopped by a local policeman.

"Are you going to Liz Fraser's party, Mr Hill?" he asked.

Benny could barely believe it.

"Miss Fraser's place is just up the road there on the left," continued the policeman. "You can't miss it."

For years afterwards people would come up to me and sat they'd never forgotten that party of mine. It was a very happy occasion. Even happier was my sale of the bungalow not long afterwards, when it fetched over £9,000. I'd paid off the loan and now could move on in my life. As a cash buyer I purchased a large ground-floor flat near Bishops Avenue.

* * *

The 'I'm Free' party was the end of an era in several ways. It obviously marked my final release from Peter but it was also one of the last times I saw Tony Hancock and Sid James together. They'd made the last couple of series of *Hancock's Half Hour* and, as per usual, I popped up regularly in those. But for Tony and Sid it was the end of the road.

There was never any argument between them. As I saw it, they were the best of friends. But professionally Tony felt he was being pigeonholed alongside Sid as a double act. He was determined to move on – even if, by doing so, their friendship was sacrificed. Which of course it was. The sad thing was that Tony never took Sid aside and explained why he'd been dropped. He just informed the BBC and that was that.

For Ray Galton and Alan Simpson this meant writing a new solo series for Tony and another one for Sid. So Tony went off to make *Hancock* while Sid, me and Bill Kerr (a veteran of Tony's radio shows) were put into *Citizen James*. I was cast as Sid's fiancée, who he's always borrowing money from, and I was delighted that Sid wanted me in the series. There was a lot of speculation in the press about whether he was a strong enough actor and a strong enough comedy character to carry his own show. Well, of course he was – on both counts.

It turned out to be an excellent series, carefully written by Ray and Alan to play to Sid's strengths. Subsequently they passed the show on to other writers; this and the fact that I was preoccupied with films meant that Sydney Tafler came in for the second series as 'feed' to Sid. I did do one of the later episodes but as a completely different character – which is either a testament to my remarkable versatility or a sign that I'd completely failed to leave my mark on the first series!

I liked Sydney Tafler a lot. The last time I saw him was at Sandown for a Variety Club event in the late 1970s. He came over to me and said, "Well, goodbye Liz. I'm dying."

"What?" I replied. "Don't be ridiculous."

"Yes I am, Liz," he said. "I've got cancer. I've only got a couple of weeks."

Sure enough, he died soon afterwards.

* * *

I may have gone into Sid's new TV show in 1960 rather than Tony's, but I liked both of them and didn't want to take sides. I couldn't anyway, because that same year I was signed up to appear in two films more or less simultaneously. One starred Tony, the other starred Sid.

The one with Tony was *The Rebel* and it was directed by Robert Day, who'd made *Two Way Stretch*. I had a cough-and-a-spit role as a surly coffee shop waitress and it was very nostalgic really – almost as if *I'm All Right Jack* had never happened. It was just one day and I did it as a favour to Tony, because I loved him dearly.

I had a dreadful hacking cough during that day on *The Rebel*, which made Tony very nervous.

"You haven't got whooping cough, have you?" he asked.

"No, of course not, Tony," I replied. "Let's just get on with the scene."

As a matter of fact, I think I *did* have whooping cough.

The film with Sid was a delight from start to finish. It was nothing out of the ordinary, really – shot in black-and-white in around six weeks and with a crop of familiar comedy faces. Still, *Double Bunk* remains my personal favourite among all the films I made.

For a start, I got on tremendously well with the three other leads, and I think it shows in the finished film. There was Sid obviously, plus Ian Carmichael, whom I knew very well, and the delightful Janette Scott. She's the daughter of Thora Hird and a more beautiful and talented actress you couldn't have hoped to meet.

The supporting actors were all so perfectly cast they could have played their roles in their sleep. There were people I knew well like Irene Handl and Dennis Price, together with some faces new to me like Naunton Wayne and Miles Malleson. I'd seen *The Lady Vanishes* and all those other films Naunton had made with Basil Radford, and now here I was playing a scene with him!

The director was Cyril Pennington-Richards, who was nice and friendly and did a really good job. He was tremendous fun and always encouraged us to have fun as well.

The weather was glorious and the locations were beautiful. We'd all clamber abroad this house boat and just go down the river a bit – shoot a scene – stop – go down the river a bit further – then shoot another one. It was like a paid holiday. The script was excellent, too, and it was a very happy film to make. Also, in my opinion, the funniest film I ever did.

Another reason I loved that film was because it involved spending a lot of time with Sid. I think the filming went some way towards easing his disappointment with Tony's decision – a decision, remember, that he didn't hear from Tony himself but from the BBC.

Sid and I had a really warm and friendly relationship. He liked to give his favourite girls pet names and mine was Lizzle. He was very sweet and soppy that way. We'd have a laugh and a cuddle; nothing lustful, just affectionate. I've never had that with any other man in my life. We were pretty much inseparable on that film.

Sid and I were almost turned into pop stars for *Double Bunk*. Well, we made a recording of the title song anyway. It was my first and only single. We recorded it in Twickenham and I thought it was great fun. It wasn't a hit, but our dulcet tones are still there over the opening credits of the film itself so it certainly isn't forgotten. It was a lovely experience and Sid's trademark laugh at the end always makes me smile.

To boost the film, in October 1960 Sid and I were interviewed for the *Sunday Pictorial*, the gist of the article – very tongue in cheek, of course – being that Sid had no interest in scantily clad girls.

"Why don't you go and lie down in your dressing room, Sid, if you're tired?" I said. "After all, you're not wanted in these scenes when I'm doing my strip sequence."

Sid explained that unclothed girls in films were a bore. "Now they've got that good actress Liz Fraser at it," he complained, adding that he preferred it when something was left to the imagination.

"Well, you could have fooled me," I replied. "You were resting your eyes about three feet out of their sockets when I was shooting that last scene."

By this time, of course, a bit of publicity about me getting down to my bra and panties was enough to attract a lot of people to the cinema. And I have to admit, I do look good in that film. I suppose that's one of the main reasons why *Double Bunk* is my favourite picture. It always helps if you look particularly glamorous – and, my goodness, I was slim.

At the very end of the film, incidentally, *Double Bunk* also has Dick Bentley and June Whitfield in it – their voices anyway, playing their famous radio characters of Ron and Eth from *Take It From Here*. These days, June, as well as being an OBE and CBE, is also my best friend.

* * *

Citizen James was a big hit for Sid but there was something even bigger just around the corner for him – and me, for that matter.

Late in 1960, Sid and I had no sooner finished *Double Bunk* than we were back in harness together at Pinewood Studios for *Carry On Regardless*. I had no idea then that I was becoming part of the most famous comedy team in British cinema history, but I suppose at this stage in my career it was a natural progression.

I may have been new to the team but they certainly weren't new to me. Sid I knew well of course, and Joan Sims too. Charles

Hawtrey I remembered from the pictures he'd made during the war with Will Hay. In fact, *Oh, Mr Porter!* was one of my favourite films; Charles wasn't in that one, I know, but the fact he'd worked with the great Will Hay was still very impressive. And I'd admired Kenneth Connor and Kenneth Williams – Joan too – in all the West End revues they'd done.

There wasn't one member of the Carry On gang you couldn't like. And they were all so efficient. They'd get to the studio, they'd know their lines, they'd say them, and then they'd go home. There was never an argument or a tantrum. It was a very happy atmosphere.

Kenneth Williams was a remarkable man, and incredibly funny – more so than any stand-up comedian. He may have been a loner but he was also a great raconteur. I could listen to his stories for hours, and frequently did. A lot of the others would be quite subdued when they weren't 'on', but not Kenneth. Though he tended to ignore anyone who didn't interest him, he could be quite sharp with people and didn't suffer fools gladly. (Then again, neither did Sid.) Kenneth was outrageous all the time, whether he was delivering bitingly witty barbs or simply breaking wind to popular show tunes.

The director, Gerald Thomas, was not only a lovely man but also a consummate professional. We never did more than one or two takes; with Gerald, we didn't need to. He was astute enough to get actors together who could do what he wanted, generally on the first take, and in the meantime he worked out all his camera shots well in advance, before any of us even turned up. That was the real secret of the Carry On films – the reason they were made so quickly and efficiently. Without a solid central figure like Gerald no film could be made in so short a period of time.

Carry On Regardless remains my favourite Carry On; it's a very funny film. I had a scene in it with Jimmy Thompson in which I had to try on all the clothes he'd bought as an anniversary gift for his wife. When the wife unexpectedly comes home, I finally emerge from the wardrobe disguised as a man. There were three or four costume changes involved, not to mention several pages of dialogue, yet that scene didn't take more than a day to shoot. In fact, now I come to think of it we shot it in half a day because I remember doing another scene with Sid in the afternoon. Nowadays that one scene might need a whole week. But not for Gerald Thomas.

The schedule on the Carry Ons was so precise that, maybe two weeks into shooting, an invitation would go up on the notice board, announcing that the end-of-picture party was going to take place at 6.30 pm on such-and-such a Friday. And invariably it would. There was never any nonsense of the kind we'd had with Basil Dearden on *Desert Mice*. Because we were a team who all knew and liked each other we did the job quickly and did the job well. Most of us had worked together before, and there wasn't one of us who wasn't experienced in television, and that was the discipline you needed to make a feature film so quickly and professionally. And with Gerald we never felt any pressure at all.

Clearly I fitted in nicely with Gerald's working methods because the following spring I was back with him and producer Peter Rogers for *Raising the Wind*. This one wasn't officially part of the Carry On series but otherwise it was much the same. Even Sid was in it, though I didn't get to see him. His small scene was probably filmed while I was on a ten-minute tea break. They worked that fast.

It was a very funny and classy film and, again, the cast were all chums – not just the Carry On people but also Leslie Phillips and James Robertson Justice from *Doctor in Love*. So I thoroughly enjoyed making it. In fact, *Raising the Wind* features one of my favourite scenes from any of my films – and it's a scene I'm not even in! I did see it being shot, however, and I really had to choke back the laughter.

In it, Kenneth Williams has to conduct a professional orchestra through 'The William Tell Overture', and his range of supercilious facial expressions is hilarious. Then, of course, he has to watch

Clockwise from top: Dad, Mum, my brother and me.

Left: My father's final birthday message to me, 1941.

My first professional photo (top left), plus various other 1950s publicity shots. I've come on a bit since then!

One day's work with Joan Sims, Gladys Henson and Harry Secombe in *Davy*, 1957.
I later became friends with them all.

Playing a Teddy Girl in *Dixon of Dock Green*, 1957.
They don't make suits like that any more!

Photographed by Peter Sellers, 1957.
No, Peter – I will not take my top off!

As the Matron in *Whack-O!* in 1957. Chiselbury School – 'for the sons of gentlefolk'.

With Ian Carmichael during the making of *I'm All Right Jack* in 1959. What a delightful man.

Above: Making sheet music with Ian in *I'm All Right Jack*. Not my own hair.

Right: Publicising *I'm All Right Jack*. Is that me?

The Kites. With dear Irene Handl and Peter Sellers in *I'm All Right Jack*.

With Reginald Beckwith and Irene Handl in *Desert Mice*. Magician's assistant!

Looking over the diamonds with David Lodge, Bernard Cribbins, Peter Sellers and Irene Handl in *Two Way Stretch*, 1959. Can I have these?

Above: With Peter in *Two Way Stretch*. Making sure his hand isn't free.

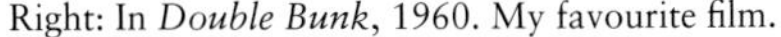

Above right: With Norman Wisdom in *The Bulldog Breed*, 1960. OK Norman – just a short walk.

Right: In *Double Bunk*, 1960. My favourite film.

Below: With Brian Rix in *The Night We Dropped a Clanger*, 1959. Commonly known nowadays as Lord Rix.

Left and above: My two favourite stars. With Sid James in *Carry On Regardless* in 1960, and with Tony Hancock at the premiere of *The Guns of Navarone* in 1961.

Below: With Graham Stark in *Watch It, Sailor!* in 1961. What did you say your name was?

aghast as the orchestra – paying him back for his rudeness to them – runs out of his control and goes completely berserk.

The plot involved Jimmy Thompson, Paul Massie, Leslie Phillips, Jennifer Jayne and myself as music students competing for a big scholarship. To my absolute amazement I was the winner! We all learned to mime playing our instruments (mine was a cello) and it looks very convincing in the finished film. I don't know which cellist played my parts but, whoever it was, I thank them very much for making me sound so good.

Shortly before making *Raising the Wind*, I'd been in a picture for Hammer Films, though sadly not one of their celebrated horrors. It was called *Watch It, Sailor!* and had Vera Day as a flustered bride and me as her best friend and bridesmaid. Dennis Price, Graham Stark, Irene Handl and Frankie Howerd were also in it, together with that wonderful old pro Bobby Howes.

When the picture was made, I'd just got back from a trip to Uruguay. Along with Leslie Phillips and Mary Peach I'd been part of the British Delegation at the Punta del Este International Film Festival. I'd had a wonderful week of fun and sun – despite the fact that British Airways lost my suitcase and I had no decent clothes to wear. I'd also ignored all the warnings about ultra-violet rays and had sat in the sun for too long. So when I got back to Britain I had big, unsightly blisters all over my lips. The people at Hammer were horrified, but the director, Wolf Rilla, got around the problem by shooting my entire performance in profile.

Mary Peach was in another film I made in 1961. *A Pair of Briefs* was a courtroom comedy from the producer-director team of Betty Box and Ralph Thomas, for whom I'd done *Doctor in Love* the previous year. Betty, incidentally, was the wife of Carry On producer Peter Rogers and Ralph was Gerald Thomas' elder brother.

There were lots of other familiar faces in it – Michael Craig and James Robertson Justice, again, from *Doctor in Love*, plus Bill Kerr from *Citizen James* and also Joan Sims. But almost all my time on set was spent with Ron Moody, who was being brilliant as always.

I was playing his girlfriend – yet another glamorous blonde only this time I had an annoying and near-constant laugh, which kept breaking out during a court case brought against him by his wife.

* * *

It was around this time that a Canadian journalist called Clyde Gilmour came over to London to interview me for the *Toronto Telegram*. Under the title 'Meet a Funny-Sexy Girl', he gave me a very nice write-up. In fact, I was so flattered I stored the article away.

> Film actresses who can be simultaneously amusing and alluring on the screen have always been in lamentably short supply on both sides of the Atlantic ... The droll and fetching wenches who somehow manage to seem funny and sexy at the same time ... are the merry temptresses of the movies. The late Carole Lombard was a member of this select sorority. So was Britain's captivating clown-princess, the late Kay Kendall. Lucille Ball also possessed the same beguiling combination ... By and large, however, it's a small and discouraging roster. I take pleasure therefore in officially nominating, as an eminent new addition to this sisterhood, a demure and rollicking Londoner named Liz Fraser who is, in my respectful opinion, much funnier than most of the sexy girls and much sexier than most of the funny ones.

I was certainly allowed to be sexy and funny in *Carry On Cruising*, which was the first of the series to be filmed in colour and took me back to Pinewood first thing in 1962. I've always loved working at Pinewood. The studios have beautiful grounds, with lawns and ponds and flowers. A little Chelsea Flower Show and so relaxing when you're off set.

It was great to be back with the familiar gang, though Charles Hawtrey was nowhere to be seen, having recently incurred the wrath of producer Peter Rogers. He'd not only demanded more money (unthinkable!) but had even requested a star on his dressing room door (ridiculous!). Lance Percival stood in for him. Joan Sims was missing due to other commitments, so they brought in Dilys Laye, who did an excellent job. In fact, I thought we made a very good team as two young secretaries on the razzle aboard the good ship SS Happy Wanderer.

It was great to spend some time with Esma Cannon while making *Carry On Cruising*. She'd flitted in and out of *I'm All Right Jack* as Margaret Rutherford's maid, and she'd been in a couple of group scenes with me in *Carry On Regardless*. But now we had lots of very funny scenes together. She was a lovely little lady and what was most endearing about her were the little glimpses you got into her family life. One day, for example, she came into the studio carrying a present from her husband.

"Oh," I said. "What was that for?"

"Well," she replied, "it's our son's birthday today and every year we always give each other a present because we feel that *we* deserve a present as well as him."

That was such a lovely idea, I thought.

It was during the *Carry On Cruising* shoot that Sid and I heard about *Play It Cool*, a film being made on the next stage by a new young director called Michael Winner. We'd been told he was yelling at everyone through a megaphone, just like an old-time Hollywood director, and that his leading lady, Anna Palk, was in tears all the time. So we crept onto the Winner stage and watched the filming from up in the gantry. It was so different from the atmosphere on the *Cruising* set! We gratefully sneaked out again.

Alas, unlike the lovely locations for my previous nautical comedy *Double Bunk*, the ship in *Carry On Cruising* never moved. We never saw a real boat at any time because a huge cruise liner set had been constructed at Pinewood, complete with a swimming pool. Though I couldn't swim, I had to get into this very deep pool and pretend I could. My style was basically to fling my arms about and hope for the best.

In the film, Dilys and I were continually popping up on the ship's balcony, waving or doing some deck game or other. We had loads of different costume changes and had to look over the rails, gazing at the ocean and at various countries on the horizon. In reality we were just looking at the blank wall of the sound stage.

"Ooh look! Corfu!" we'd shout. There was nothing there!

CHAPTER SIX

Dinner with Peter and Judy

Since divorcing Peter Yonwin I hadn't dated anyone. I'd had plenty of offers but couldn't work up any enthusiasm. In the end it was that ludicrous Star House Tin Foil ad that led to my meeting my second husband. Ian Fordyce turned out to be a man of his word, for he did use me on several occasions after that memorable day and it was through him that I got my first part in *No Hiding Place*.

That was back in 1959, and over the next few years I appeared in several more episodes of the show. As a result, I met and worked with Ian's very good friend at Associated-Rediffusion, the director Bill Hitchcock. Apparently we'd met years before when Bill was a callboy and I was an extra, but I had no memory of that. But as soon as I saw him to discuss a new *No Hiding Place* episode I knew that I would never forget him.

These weren't live broadcasts any more; they were recorded on tape instead. Unfortunately, it was still like doing it live because the tape cost so much money and edits were frowned upon. Gone were the days of the cut-key so fluffed lines just went in regardless.

It was Sid James, incidentally, who told me the secret to getting a re-take. If you made a mistake and you really wanted to do it again you just had to say "Fuck!" and then they'd *have* to take it again. Your fellow actors might not be best pleased but at least you'd made sure your mistake wouldn't be seen by millions of TV viewers. In one episode of *No Hiding Place* that Bill directed me in, a detective slammed a door and the glass shattered! He just continued as if nothing had happened. To me, that was a "Fuck!" moment if ever there was one.

I was very impressed with Bill. Not only was he a brilliant director but he was a very charming man. He was also very married. On top of this, he had a reputation as a ladies' man; in fact, he'd had a string of affairs, generally with his personal assistants. So I was determined not to get involved.

I got involved almost immediately.

It all seemed very odd to me. I was newly divorced and he was a married man who wasn't planning on leaving his wife. So I felt a little uneasy about his interest in me. He asked me out to dinner several times. He'd take me to Rules in Covent Garden and other restaurants, but I had no wish to have an affair with a married man, which was against all my principles.

I was filming *A Pair of Briefs* at the time. The location for the courtroom scenes was Lincoln's Inn, which was just around the corner from Rediffusion, where Bill was shooting an episode of *No Hiding Place*. So I'd go along in my breaks to watch him direct.

I realised then that I had never loved my first husband. But I'd fallen very much in love with Bill Hitchcock.

* * *

Curiously enough, another serial womaniser reappeared in my life at this very same time.

It was 1962 and I was appearing in *The Amorous Prawn* at Shepperton. I hadn't worked with Peter Sellers since *Two Way Stretch* but now he was on another sound stage shooting *The Dock Brief*. It was exactly the same as before. Every time he saw me he'd say, "How about joining me for lunch in my dressing room?"

I felt much more confident by this time so, much to his surprise, I called his bluff and said, "Great. Just lunch, Peter."

"Yes, of course," he said. "It's just lunch."

Well, I arrived at his dressing room and he invited me in. No lunch! Instead, he locked the door and whipped off his trousers. I remained calm and thought fast. The only way I could get out of the situation – and not arouse Peter's vindictive nature – was to tell him that I found him very attractive but that I couldn't participate because I knew his wife Anne so well *and* I would get hurt.

It was complete rubbish but it did the trick. Peter reluctantly put his trousers back on, unlocked the door and calmly ordered his usual light lunch of Ryvita, cheese and apples. He was, as always, concerned about his weight.

We remained friends but, unfortunately for Peter, his womanising finally caught up with him and destroyed his marriage to Anne. He'd had a string of affairs and hurt a lot of people but never suffered himself. Losing Anne, though, really hurt him. He claimed to have had an affair with Sophia Loren, whom he'd starred with in *The Millionairess*. According to Peter, he was bedding Italy's most beautiful film star – and he was so pleased with himself he even told Anne. Wrong move! She threw him out.

To placate her, Peter suggested selling their house in the country and making a fresh start in London. He was going to turn over a new leaf. To that end he bought an empty property at the top of a Hampstead apartment block and told Anne to hire an architect and create her dream home. Well, she did hire an architect and then ran off with him. It was ironic, to say the least, but Peter didn't see the joke.

Soon afterwards I was at a Variety Club race meeting and was having a wonderful time with friends like Tommy Cooper, David Lodge and Davy Kaye. We all ended up at Tommy's house and he suggested the four of us go off to a West End casino. I was looking forward to this as I loved roulette. Before we left, though, the conversation had naturally turned to Peter and his problems. Although it was a secret to the general public we'd all heard about it and, frankly, we had a bit of a laugh about it. In fact, I thought it served Peter right.

David, who was the closest to Peter, suggested we telephone him and try to cheer him up – though we had to pretend, of course, that we didn't know about the split with Anne.

When it was my turn on the telephone, Peter said, "I'm on my own and it's my birthday."

He sounded very depressed and I felt genuinely sorry for him. "Look Peter," I said, "you can't spend your birthday on your own. Come out with us. We're all off to a casino, it'll be great fun."

"I can't possibly face all those people. Will you come over here?"

I didn't really want to and told him so. Peter persisted, however. "I'll take you out to a quiet restaurant I know," he said, "and we'll have a lovely dinner."

Now, if there's one thing that I really love it's good food. So I thought for a moment and then gave in. I'd traded in my Ford Anglia by this time so I drove over to Peter's place in my new MGB. It was the first time I'd ever stepped over the threshold of his magnificent new Hampstead flat.

Peter wasn't exactly dressed to go out to a restaurant. In fact, he was wearing slacks and a sloppy old sweater. Still, he welcomed me into an enormous lounge, about 40 feet square, and offered me a drink.

"I thought we were going out," I said. "Are you going to put some decent clothes on?"

"We're eating in!" he replied. His manservant, apparently, was preparing a gorgeous dinner. "While we wait, would you like the guided tour?" he added.

It was a beautiful place and I was really impressed. Of course, Peter being Peter the guided tour included the bedroom. Once we got there he paused and said, "You know, we have at least an hour before dinner is ready..."

He'd tried so many times in the past and I'd half expected it. "Peter," I said, "I'm only here for the dinner."

He then started getting rather mournful about Anne and told me his version of the story, which wasn't the version I'd heard. In fact, from his point of view Anne had done him wrong. He couldn't go on without her, he said. With that he suddenly unzipped his trousers and exposed himself.

"You can put that away!" I said. And he did.

We then had another drink and carried on talking as if nothing had happened.

Among the penthouse's most fascinating features were the doors. It seemed as if there weren't any. The walls would just slide open to reveal this manservant, who then served the dinner. It was very disconcerting; you never knew when the wall would just open up to reveal him.

I'll always remember what we ate. I'm not likely to forget any detail of that extraordinary evening. The first course was a delicious lobster bisque, which I ate quickly as I really wanted the evening to end. I was determined, however, to finish my dinner!

Bill had recently given me an absolutely beautiful eternity ring – blue and white diamonds and sapphires – which I wore on my wedding finger. While we were eating Peter suddenly became very curious about it. He knew I was divorced and didn't think I was with anybody because Liz Fraser never *was* with anybody.

"What's this ring?" he asked.

"Oh," I said, "I've met somebody, Peter, and I love him dearly."

There was a really long pause. I continued to tuck into the soup but the conversation had completely frozen. After what seemed like minutes Peter said, "I think you'd better go."

"What?" I said.

"I think you'd better go," he replied. "I can't see any point in your staying."

"I'm not going anywhere," I said, "until I've had my dinner."

I was so angry. I said, "Look Peter, I could have had an evening at a casino. What I'm not going to do is leave without having my dinner. I came round here because it was your birthday and you were on your own. Not only have you behaved inappropriately but you're now going back on your promise."

He didn't say another word. The manservant came in, took away the empty soup plates, and then brought in steaks with asparagus, mushrooms and potatoes. This was followed by strawberries and cream. I ate the entire meal in silence.

When I'd finished I said, "Thank you very much for a lovely dinner, Peter. And happy birthday."

He walked me to a bit of wall that turned out to be the lift down to the ground floor and that was that. At least *my* appetite was satisfied! I then went to see Tommy and the rest at the casino and won ten pounds.

Soon afterwards, Peter became heavily involved with the top clairvoyant Maurice Woodruff, who told Peter he'd meet and marry someone with the initials BE. Britt Ekland then arrived in Britain and the rest is history.

As for Peter, our one and only meeting after the Hampstead dinner was some time in the early 1970s, maybe ten years later. We were both doing different programmes at the ATV studios at Borehamwood and Peter had his son Michael with him. We spoke as if nothing had happened. I retained a grudging fondness for him; he could be awful but there was something about him I liked.

When he died in 1980, the first I heard about it was when I was phoned by the television people, who wanted me to come on and speak about him. They were putting together an obituary for Peter and were going to use a clip of us together in *Two Way Stretch* – the very scene he'd tried to throw away all those years before. I was very shocked to hear the news. It was awful, but at least we'd patched up any lingering awkwardness.

* * *

The Amorous Prawn was a fun film. It was based on a big West End hit written by Anthony Kimmins, who also directed the film version; in fact, I went along to see the play before we started shooting. I was back with Dennis Price and Ian Carmichael, this time with the added bonus of Cecil Parker and Joan Greenwood. Joan, in particular, I was very thrilled to work with. She was such a precise, delicate and perfect actress.

My big chum on set, of course, was Ian Carmichael, who was one of my favourite leading men. He was a complete professional and great company, too, when we headed off on a promotional tour for the film. We travelled all over the place. To while away the time on all the train journeys, we'd play Scrabble together, for money. I won every game and Ian would often be searching for loose change.

The Amorous Prawn came out in late November 1962, but by that time the taste for straightforward British comedies of the kind I'd been making was on the wane. On top of that, I'd noticed a pattern. It was hard to miss, really. I'd made 20 feature films in just under four years, and in a lot of them I'd shed quite a lot of my clothes. In *The Amorous Prawn*, for example, I'd stripped down to bra and panties again.

"I shall put up a fierce fight against undressing in future," I told the press.

* * *

When *The Amorous Prawn* was released, I was just heading off on maybe the most exciting trip of my life – to Mexico.

I spent several weeks there enjoying the food, surf and sun – oh, and promoting British films, which is what I'd been sent over to do. Along with my *Raising the Wind* co-star Jennifer Jayne, I'd been asked to go to Acapulco to represent the British film industry. So we went over with a Lord and Lady Something-or-Other on behalf of Great Britain. We had a fabulous time. I particularly enjoyed having drinks out of scooped-out pineapples. I could have got very used to that.

Because I couldn't swim, I wasn't keen to join in the water-skiing, which everybody was having a go at it with the aid of the local Mexican boys. Most people tended to fall off when they first got on the skis, so I thought the same would happen to me and that would be that.

"Well," I said to myself, "I won't even get started."

To my horror, however, I found that I *did* stay on the skis. There was a Mexican boy skiing beside me and before I knew it I was being towed into the Gulf of Mexico. We passed three warships and, though still staying upright on the skis, I was petrified that the belt of corks wouldn't be any use if I fell in. I did indeed fall in but was quickly pulled into the boat. That experience should have forced me to learn to swim but it didn't. I still can't, and won't!

All the films in the festival were shown in the open air, with a fireworks display each evening. It was obviously difficult for me to follow some of the foreign-language films. I remember seeing Ingmar Bergman's *The Virgin Spring*. Much later I caught it again, this time with subtitles, and realised that I'd misinterpreted the whole plot. About halfway through the Acapulco screening I'd started to make up my own story!

Each country had its own film entry and gala evening. The American one was wonderfully lavish and over the top. The worst by far was the British one. It was so conservative and was certainly the stingiest; all we served were sandwiches and tit-bits! The host nation, of course, had a reputation to keep up, so the Mexican evening was particularly spectacular and boasted the biggest firework display of the whole festival.

Cantiflas was the guest of honour that evening. He was Mexico's Charlie Chaplin and I vividly remember meeting him. He was a very charming man and gave me a doll in national dress as a memento of my stay. I still have it.

Having watched the Mexican film we sat down to eat, but then the evening took a nasty turn. Somebody cleared a space on the floor and started putting sand down. I turned to the English ambassador.

"What's happening now?" I asked.

"They're about to have a cock fight," he replied.

"I can't stay for that!"

"But you have to," he said. "They are our hosts. Protocol and all that. You can't leave."

So I left.

I went to the loo and waited. I'd been in there quite long enough for the two cockerels to have dismembered each other when another lady came in. She was dark and very beautiful – obviously from Brazil or Argentina or somewhere. I said to her, "Have they finished?" Not unnaturally she didn't understand a word. "Parlez-vous Français?" I ventured. That seemed to get some sort of reaction so I said, "Avez les poulets fini la guerre?" Which roughly translated meant "Have they finished the chicken war?" She nodded, so I went back to the main room just in time to see all the bloodied sand being swept up. Thankfully, I had missed it all.

I didn't miss the earthquake though. That was our most extraordinary experience in Mexico. I was sitting outside the hotel with Lord and Lady Thing and the ground started to shake. After a while it became more and more violent. We looked at each other and I said, "This must happen all the time."

We were facing the sea and there was no beach. The water was only about ten feet away and of course I couldn't swim. The building started shaking and it was only when all the staff started running out of the hotel and into the sea that we realised we were in the middle of quite a nasty earthquake. Jennifer, meanwhile, was in her room and had realised there was a problem when all her make-up things rolled off her dressing table.

Despite all the panic, my friends and I just sat there. In fact, I remember writing a postcard to someone at home and saying, very matter of factly, "Oh, I've just been in an earthquake."

Britain won the Gold prize for Best Film. That was *A Kind of Loving* with Alan Bates and June Ritchie, so it was certainly justified. As a representative of the British film industry I was asked if I'd bring the award back into the country. I had to smuggle it in and I didn't declare it. I thought it was *real* gold!

* * *

I remember I'd just finished *Carry On Cruising* when my agent, John Redway, said to me, "Look Liz, if you keep on doing these Carry On films I'll never be able to get you any other work." Another thing he said was, "Once you get star billing you can never take anything less. So do you consider yourself a leading lady or are you a character actress?"

That was very clever of him. And he was right, of course. In fact, the film I'd picked up an award for in Acapulco was a case in point. *A Kind of Loving* was June Ritchie's first picture, and she took star billing in it. But she then made only a few more films (in fact, I was in one of them – *Live Now Pay Later*) and after that was gone.

Of course, I knew perfectly well that I was a character actress. A series like *Citizen James* had suited me down to the ground for that very reason – because I was always content to be part of the supporting team. Offers had flooded in after *I'm All Right Jack*, and there was talk of me having my own comedy series on television. But I didn't want to be a star and, except for my stage work in later years, never went above the title.

Actually, John and I had already had a go at breaking the comedy mould *and* taking top billing. He'd fixed up a very cheaply made film for me, a B picture really, called *The Painted Smile*. Hardly anybody has heard of it, and even fewer have actually seen it – thank goodness. But it was an interesting film for me to do at that time. I was cast as a nightclub hostess who gets into difficulty with the various vicious men she encounters.

As things turned out, it was a disaster. The director was Lance Comfort, who gave me a little pre-production pep talk that did my self-confidence no good at all.

"Before we start shooting," he said, "there are several things you should bear in mind. You are an established comedy actress and this is not a funny part."

Well, I knew that.

I had "all these comedy traits," apparently. "You have this walk," he said. "It's a funny walk and I'd like you to think about changing it. Concentrate on getting rid of that funny wiggling walk you have."

"Right," I said. "I really hadn't realised that."

"And then there are your eyes," he continued. "You move your eyes around a lot when you say your lines. You have these big comedy eyes."

"Right..."

"And then there's your mouth. You do this very strange thing with your mouth when you say your lines. You sort of twist it around."

"I do?"

"Yes you do," he assured me.

So that was my eyes, mouth and walk accounted for. I thought I may as well just get up and go home. But he hadn't finished yet.

"Then, of course, there's your voice."

"My voice?" I replied, getting more demoralised by the minute. "What's wrong with my voice?"

"Well," he said, "you have this very squeaky, high-pitched comedy voice. I'd like you to try and correct that."

All this was dumped on me on the first day of filming. I pretty much had to pick myself up from the floor and go straight into my first scene with my handsome co-star Peter Reynolds. Anyway, I got through the shoot somehow. At least, being such a low-budget film, it was a very quick schedule – something like two or three weeks.

My agent and I went along to a preview theatre in Wardour Street to see the finished film. As my first dramatic – and starring – role this apparently marked a change for the better in my career. The screening room went dark, the film started and there I was, sitting on the side of a bed and putting on my stockings. OK, so I was still acting in my bra and panties but at least this was a serious role.

Then there came out of the screen this stilted, very low-pitched voice. "Mark! Mark! I'm not coming!" It was terrible.

We both sneaked out of the screening room and John said, "Well, we won't do that again, will we?"

And I never did.

It was Lance Comfort's fault really. He'd made me feel so self-conscious and it's never a good thing when you're trying too hard on a film set. With that camera pointing at you, every little thing is magnified.

As with most dreadful things that have happened in my life I quickly blocked *The Painted Smile* from my mind. About 20 years later, however, Roy Hudd asked me to be a guest on his TV show *Movie Memories* – and, lo and behold, somehow they'd dug up a clip from *The Painted Smile*. By that time, of course, I was able to have a good laugh about how bad it was. And as they were screening the clip I noticed a young actor hovering in the background whom I hadn't even remembered being in the film. It was David Hemmings.

Then just a few years ago the film was screened in its entirety on television at some godforsaken hour in the early morning, so I decided to sit down and watch it for the first time since that harrowing Wardour Street screening. I had another surprise in store. I'd forgotten that I died at the end of the film. But there I was, being chased through a quarry by Kenneth Griffith and being shot dead! I had no memory of filming that scene at all.

The Painted Smile was a brave try that nobody saw. *Live Now Pay Later* was another matter; in fact, it's a film I'm very proud of. Having told the press that I was going to move away from the bra and panties stuff after finishing *The Amorous Prawn*, I did just that in this new picture. Unfortunately, the films were released in reverse order, so that just weeks after praising my performance in *Live Now Pay Later* the critics were moaning about my having taken the easy option again in *The Amorous Prawn*.

Well, it's purely academic now but with *Live Now Pay Later* I really did try to change my career on my own terms. There was no Lance Comfort discomfort on *this* film; the director was Jay Lewis and, though a comedy, it was a very different kind of comedy. Certainly my performance was different. I was playing an ordinary, downtrodden housewife who's married to Geoffrey Keen and is desperate to impress her husband's bosses. So she gets into huge debt and tries to conceal the evidence from her snobbish husband. In the end, she throws herself under a bus.

"That's more like it," I thought. "Committing suicide... Real acting!"

* * *

It was also in 1962 that I got to meet one of my biggest heroes.

The legendary Judy Garland was in town to make *I Could Go On Singing* with Dirk Bogarde and to perform a number of live concerts in the capital. I was very friendly with the publicist Theo Cowan and one day he asked if I'd like to join him and Judy for dinner – just the three of us. Would I? It was an absolute thrill.

A car was sent for me and we had a pre-dinner drink in a club somewhere in Piccadilly. We moved on to another club where, on her entrance, the resident quartet started playing 'Somewhere Over the Rainbow'. At the end they all looked towards her with respectful nods, yet she didn't acknowledge them.

"Aren't you going to thank them?" I whispered.

"They can all fuck off!" she said to me. "I'm sick of the fucking thing."

I was absolutely shocked by this but later on I understood how she felt – everywhere she went people would start playing 'Somewhere Over the Rainbow' and it must have driven her mad.

Then we started talking about her upcoming film and Shepperton Studios, where she was due to shoot it. I had, of course, spent a lot of my career on those sound stages and she was keen to know about the place.

"Your greatest fans work at Shepperton," I told her. "They're called Chuck and Bobby and they've been the prop men at the studio for years."

"Really?" drawled Judy.

"Yes," I said. "Virtually their whole lives have been built around being fans of yours. It'll be the most exciting thing ever for them, you coming to work there."

I didn't find out until several years later, but during the making of the film she sacked the pair of them. They were just so over-awed by her being there she became absolutely sick of it. The actor Mark Eden later co-wrote a little radio play about the incident, called *Props*.

Anyway, Judy Garland was my idol and I got to have dinner with her. It remains a precious memory.

CHAPTER SEVEN

Where's My Mouse?

By the end of 1962 I was keen to get back to the stage. Right then I was offered a James Saunders play called *Next Time I'll Sing to You* at the Arts Theatre, little knowing that it would go on to win an *Evening Standard* award for Best Drama.

I was the only woman in a cast of five; the character was called Lizzie. It was a very odd play of two separate halves, in which we all just sat or stood around and talked a lot, and we didn't really understand what it was all about. I was determined to make a success of it, though – I thought it was very challenging and 'of the moment'. It was certainly more interesting than just standing around in a bikini all day, as I'd been doing for so many years. I was still playing the silly blonde type that I'd played on screen, but I was able to do something different with it.

A fellow actor from the Elephant and Castle, Michael Caine, was also in the cast. Although he'd been understudying for Peter O'Toole in *The Long and the Short and the Tall* he was essentially a film and television actor, like me. Because our route through TV and bit parts in films had been similar we tackled the play in the same way.

It was also because of our track record in films and TV that we were somewhat looked down upon by the so-called 'proper' actors in the company – though, during rehearsals at the Arts Theatre, Michael Bryant, Barry Foster and Denys Graham admitted that they didn't know what the play was about either. There were a lot of non-sequiturs involved but we somehow managed to learn our lines (and more or less understand them) by the time we opened in the last week of January 1963.

The play was almost completely composed of monologues in which we'd just talk to the audience. I had a particularly long one at the beginning of Act Two – just over three pages of dialogue. I've no idea how I managed to remember it but I've found out since that it's become something of a classic. For years afterwards I would meet producers who'd say, "The number of times I've had girls come along and do that speech of yours as their audition piece!"

It lasted about five minutes and I'd walk off the stage each night to a huge round of applause. Then Michael, who was terrific, began a long speech of his own immediately afterwards, asking whether there were any undertakers in the house – murderers? ironmongers? etc. It was that sort of play.

Harold Hobson of the *Sunday Times* called it "profound and poetic and uproariously ribald and funny" and virtually every other theatre critic followed suit. So it came as no surprise when we transferred to a much larger theatre, the Criterion, in February.

* * *

Michael was sharing a flat at the time with Terence Stamp and his current 'bird', the lovely Edina Ronay. Michael was quite jealous of Terence's success. I think this spurred him on; he just wanted to be more successful than his flat-mate, but in a friendly way as they were great chums.

Soon enough we heard that the play was due to be transferred to Broadway. To find out how we'd get on, I went to see a clairvoyant I knew called Rose Nash, who lived near the Spurs football ground in north London. The other cast members were intrigued, too, so they each gave me a personal item to take with me. Michael gave me a ring, Barry a pen and so forth.

I made sure, of course, not to tell Rose about our New York trip, yet she claimed that we were all due to leave the country in the near future. "She's so right," I thought.

Then she said that the one who owned the ring – Michael – was going to travel across deserts to a very strange place. Bit odd, I thought. Then the pen told her that Barry was also going away but would be surrounded by very tall buildings. Well, that sounded more like it – Broadway! And for me she predicted that I'd go somewhere in America and that when I got to the airport I'd remember her and send her a postcard. So, apart from the odd bit about Michael, everything seemed to be pointing towards Broadway.

What subsequently happened was this. American Equity ruled that they couldn't allow an all-British cast. There was some kind of exchange programme in those days – two American to two British or something like that – and the play simply wouldn't have worked with a mixed cast.

Despite the Broadway run falling through, all Rose Nash's predictions actually came true. In October, Barry got to play Broadway in the double-bill of *The Private Ear and The Public Eye*. At the same time, I went off to MGM in Hollywood (of which more later). And as for Michael Caine... He went to South Africa!

Next Time I'll Sing to You was certainly a play to be noticed in. It was on everyone's list and one of the celebrities who came to see it was Stanley Baker, who was casting for his upcoming film *Zulu*. He loved the play and saw potential in Michael in particular. Michael was duly invited to meet Stanley and the film's director Cy Endfield, but he was very nervous about the meeting and asked to borrow my mouse.

Pride of place in my dressing room at the Criterion went to a little grey furry mouse, a lucky mascot that my brother bought for me from Fortnum & Mason. He had whiskers, a long tail and was even eating a piece of cheese. So Michael came into my dressing room and said, "I'm seeing Stanley Baker tomorrow about this film *Zulu* and I'd like to borrow your lucky mouse."

Off he went with the mouse. He returned it the next day but only a few days later he wanted to borrow it again. The mouse was obviously working because he'd been called back for a film test and wanted the mouse with him when he did it. He didn't get the role he'd actually gone up for – the arrogant cockney eventually played by James Booth – but had got something even better – the upper-class officer Lieutenant Gonville Bromhead.

Naturally, Michael had to drop out of *Next Time I'll Sing to You*. Victor Winding came in to replace him for the remainder of our Criterion run, while Peter McEnery stepped in for Michael Bryant, who was also leaving. And very good they were too.

But Michael wasn't finished with that mouse. He was due to go off to South Africa and wanted to take it with him. "I'm quite superstitious about it now," he explained.

"What am I supposed to do without my mouse for three months?" I said. "I don't want to part with it."

"What can go wrong?" he replied. "The play's transferring to Broadway, isn't it?"

Well, I finally agreed for the mouse to leave the country, and me. And as soon as Michael went off to Africa, of course, the Broadway run was called off.

I was with a new agent by now – Dennis Selinger – and he was Michael's agent too. When I didn't hear from Michael on his return I got on the phone to Dennis to try and get my mascot back. This went on for months, with Michael saying he wanted to keep hold of it until the film was actually released.

Eventually, the premiere of *Zulu* came around and I was invited. I arrived at the Plaza in Piccadilly Circus in a beautiful blue velvet dress with a hooped skirt and matching cloak. Once inside, I found myself sitting next to – you guessed it – Michael Caine.

"Where's my bloody mouse?" I hissed.

"It's in my pocket," he said calmly.

"Give it to me," I insisted.

"You can have it back when the film has finished."

The film was a smash hit, of course. When the audience burst into applause at the end Michael turned to me and handed me back the mouse. He'd lost his whiskers and his cheese, but at least he was back with his rightful owner. So you could say that Michael Caine owes his first big success to me. And, of course, my lucky mouse.

* * *

When Michael Caine headed off to kill Zulus in South Africa, I was back at Pinewood Studios for my third Carry On film.

I'd often vowed never to make a film at the same time that I was appearing in a play. After all, I'd seen how exhausted Ian Carmichael was on the set of *The Amorous Prawn* because he was in *Critic's Choice* in the West End at the same time. But thanks to the unexpected Broadway cancellation of *Next Time I'll Sing to You*, the film was a welcome diversion during the play's London run.

I was happy to go back to working with the Carry On gang. My character was quite a tough career girl this time, keeping Kenneth Connor on his toes in their on-off romance and helping Hattie Jacques to set up an all-female cab company. And, in fact, we didn't know we were in a Carry On while filming it. The film I signed for was entitled *Call Me a Cab*. Like *Raising the Wind*, it was another Gerald Thomas-Peter Rogers comedy but not intended (initially anyway) as part of the Carry On series. On release, of course, it became *Carry On Cabby*.

The film saw the return of Charles Hawtrey to the team, after his demands regarding *Carry On Cruising* had kept him out of that film. He was a curious little man who always had his mother with him at the studio. He'd try to barricade her in his dressing room while he was working but she'd escape and run amok, throwing toilet rolls around the studio. He'd join Sid and me and the other seasoned poker players between takes but he was a hopeless player.

He never won anything but he'd bring out his little purse of coins and take the whole thing very seriously.

I can't say I ever got to know Charles very well but I suppose out of all of us he had the longest film career. I think he regretted spending the final 15 years of it making the Carry Ons. However, he was on great form in *Carry On Cabby*. As was Hattie, who was a generous and loving lady and a huge loss to us all when she suddenly died in 1980.

* * *

After *Carry On Cabby* I was still wondering about that intriguing trip to America that Rose Nash had predicted. The prediction seemed all the more peculiar because I'd never worked abroad. There had been various film industry perks, of course – the festivals in Mexico and Uruguay, and before that a ten-day tour of the USA to promote *Two Way Stretch*. I'd also opened the Globe Cinema in Tripoli with a special screening of *Doctor in Love*.

But now, in the wake of Rose's prediction, what had there been? *Carry On Cabby* at Pinewood in April. *Night of 100 Stars* at the London Palladium in July, in which I formed part of an all-star chorus line with Janette Scott, Anna Massey, Juliet and Hayley Mills, Judi Dench, Sylvia Syms, Eunice Gayson and Peggy Cummins. I'd been a guest at the Cork Film Festival in September. And now I'd been signed up to appear in *The Americanization of Emily* at the MGM Studios in Borehamwood.

Very nice, of course ... but still no sign of going to America.

I didn't realise it, but the *Emily* production team were having trouble with the technicians at MGM. They wanted to negotiate a smaller crew, but the unions, who of course were used to insisting on a four-man team to change a light bulb, refused to work on any film with fewer than 80 crew members. So MGM in America called the unions' bluff. Four days into filming, all of us actors received an unexpected call.

"Pack your bags," we were told. "We're off to Hollywood!"

It was really the beginning of the end for MGM in Britain, and the whole industry would gradually feel the knock-on effect.

I didn't know it during the flight – he was in First Class and I was in Second – but en route to Los Angeles I was on the same plane as Roger Moore. We bumped into each other at the luggage carousel and he kissed me effusively.

The baggage was wending its way around and he picked up several beautiful pieces of luggage, as befitted his status. My problem was that all I had was a tatty couple of cases tied up with string. In fact, I let them pass me by.

"I'll wait and help you with your luggage," said Roger.

"No," I replied. "You go on."

My luggage went round a second time.

"It's OK," I assured him. "Please, you go. I'm sure they'll find my cases in a minute."

He reluctantly pecked me on the cheek and left. By this time my two cases were going round on their own. Once I got back to England I quickly dumped them – though I still didn't buy any Louis Vuitton.

On arriving in LA, I recalled another part of Rose Nash's prediction. "When you get to the airport," she'd said, "you'll remember me and send me a postcard." So I did.

Funnily enough, I'd recently made a little prediction of my own, albeit with tongue very much in cheek. I was always being asked the same questions by journalists in those days and one of the most frequent was, "Do you have any ambitions left to fulfil?" My stock answer was that I'd like to play the Nurse in *Romeo and Juliet*. That was true, actually. Even so, I was getting a little fed up of saying it so one day I thought I'd change my answer.

I was passionate about poker. I was always playing it during breaks in filming, and as a result I loved watching the James Garner television series *Maverick*, in which he played a smooth, poker-playing card-shark. So on this one occasion I responded to the standard question about unfulfilled ambitions with, "Yes. I'd like to play poker with James Garner."

Well, suddenly there I was in Hollywood, filming a big-budget drama for MGM. Julie Andrews was the star and her dashing leading man was none other than James Garner. I couldn't believe it. And, yes, we did play poker in his caravan at every opportunity we could. Thankfully, on a busy film set that was a lot of the time. He was an excellent player in real life as well as on the screen. Our fellow cast member, James Coburn, also enjoyed a game so we'd play during breaks on the set. We'd play an American game called Hearts. In fact, the three of us would play cards all the time.

I stayed in a suite at the Beverly Hills Hotel and had a ball with Julie Andrews, a really lovely lady. We were shown all sorts of marvellous places around Palm Springs. All the American men loved our English accents and we were hotly pursued.

I really liked James Coburn; he was a real gentleman. There was another British actress who was fond of him too – though rather too much for some people's liking. There was quite a group of British talent over in Hollywood making this film and this particular actress was flaunting her affection for James Coburn all over the place. In fact, somehow or other some rather lurid photographs started circulating around the set.

It was Joyce Grenfell who first saw these pictures and alerted Julie and me to the situation. As the British contingent we felt this actress was bringing our nation into disrepute! So Julie went to the head of production and said that these spicy photos were being distributed around the studio and should be stopped. Subsequently the naughty actress stayed behind in America and married a millionaire, so she didn't do too badly!

Talking about my passion for poker reminds me of a major Variety Club charity event that happened around this time. It took place at a Butlin's holiday camp and all the star guests had their own chalets. In one of them there was a big poker game going on; the players were Sean Connery, Stanley Baker, Charlie Drake,

Michael Medwin and Bruce Forsyth. Sean played straight, Stanley bluffed and Charlie was just daft. So I rushed down to our chalet and woke up Bill, asking how much cash he had on him. Between us we rustled up £17-10s, so back I went to join Sean and the others.

I won just over £200 and ran back to Bill screaming, "I won! I won!"

"I knew you would," he said and promptly went back to sleep.

* * *

By the time I returned from Hollywood, the problem with the unions in the British film industry had reached fever pitch.

A huge crisis meeting of all the industry unions was called in December 1963. It was held at the Criterion Theatre, which I knew well from the recent run of *Next Time I'll Sing to You*, and my Equity card allowed me in. It was a raucous affair, with Sir Tom O'Brien, who had been knighted for his services to the industry, presiding on the stage alongside the heads of ACTT, NATKE and every other union you could think of. In the auditorium, speakers would stand up and announce themselves prior to ranting on and on.

Ever the idiot, I stood up and Sir Tom immediately bellowed "Name?"

"Liz Fraser!" I replied in my best 'projected' stage voice. "Equity!"

I wasn't sure any of these men had even heard of Equity, but I carried on.

"Look," I said. "It's the unions' fault that the industry is in the mess it's in."

I went on to outline my views on why our studios were failing, including the important fact that my latest film had been lost to Hollywood because of the intransigence of the various film unions. "It's all your fault!" I concluded.

I cannot adequately convey the incredulous silence that followed my speech. It didn't last long, however. After a pregnant pause, there was absolute uproar. I was literally boo'd out of the place.

Quite right, too. Just keep quiet, Liz!

CHAPTER EIGHT

Their Backs Were Electric!

In 1964 I made just one film – *Every Day's a Holiday*. This was a holiday camp musical, shot in Clacton-on-Sea, featuring me and Ron Moody alongside pop personalities like Freddie Garrity and Mike Sarne. The photography was particularly good; it was by Nicolas Roeg, who later directed *Don't Look Now* and lots of other films.

Either side of *Every Day's a Holiday* I had a couple of theatre engagements that were much more memorable, though not necessarily for the right reasons.

The producer Bob Swash had got hold of a black comedy by John Patrick called *Everybody Loves Opal* – 'A Prank in Three Acts,' according to the author. This was due for a short tour before going into the Vaudeville Theatre. It had a wonderful cast including Warren Mitchell, Betty Marsden and James Villiers. It was about a small gang of confidence tricksters who insure an elderly lady and then try to kill her for the insurance money.

Though well written, it was fairly standard stuff. Bob, however, was confident it would do well – which seems odd in retrospect, given that it had lasted less than three weeks on Broadway.

Betty was the old lady, Opal; Warren was the Jewish wheeler-dealer, Solomon; I was Gloria, the dizzy gangster's moll, and James was Vic, the smooth-talking leader of the gang. Perfect casting all round! But then Bob made a fatal mistake. He hired a very well-known director, who shall remain nameless.

We soon realised that this guy was very fond of giving the cast notes – all the time. We were just finding our feet on tour – we were in Torquay at the time – when he delivered the most devastating 'note' of all. He pinpointed certain lines for each actor and said, "Having received your cue you must then count to ten before saying your next line."

Well, that just left yawning great gaps between the speeches. It seemed as if we'd all forgotten our lines at certain points in the play and, inevitably, the comic rhythm of the piece was destroyed. Sometimes we couldn't help but come in with our lines before having counted to ten, but he'd come down on us like a ton of bricks. And he made it clear that he'd given us this direction because he was unhappy with our performances.

Unsurprisingly, by the time we opened at the Vaudeville we were all very bad. Somehow, the director had managed to do the impossible and make us all look terrible in roles we were perfect for – roles we could have played in our sleep in any other circumstances. The reviews, of course, were catastrophic. (Here's one from the *Daily Mail*: "Betty Marsden portrays a collector of junk. Her room is packed with rubbish – and so, I'm afraid, is the play in which she appears.") And the notice went up almost immediately. We opened on Wednesday the 1st of April (that should have been an omen) and closed on Saturday the 4th. It was one of the shortest runs in West End history.

We all felt dreadful about it. Bob, whose first producing venture this was, felt even worse. But on the last night Warren went round all the dressing rooms and told each of us that, since there was now nothing left to lose, he was going to go on stage and play his role exactly as he'd wanted to play it from the outset. So we all agreed to just go out there and act it like we all wanted to.

Betty Marsden was quite brilliant on that last night. We all were. It was great fun. It wasn't earth-shattering but it was well acted and funny. We had a terrific reaction from the very sparse audience and we came off feeling as if we'd done a good job. For that one performance, anyway.

We had a shock in store, however. Bob, the producer, came round afterwards and ripped into us because we hadn't played it that way every night. He said, "I think that you've all done the most wicked thing! It was a completely different show this evening. I've lost money and you've all let me down."

He thought we'd deliberately scuppered the play earlier in the week. However hard we tried to explain that it was the director who was at fault, he blamed us.

On a lighter note, I remember an amusing little incident from the *Everybody Loves Opal* tour. In Torquay Warren and I were sharing the same digs and one night a TV play he'd been in was due to be broadcast.

"I'm really keen to see this play," he said. "Tell you what. Let's dash back to the digs straight after the final curtain. If we're quick, we should be just in time for the start."

There was no video in those days, remember – even a repeat wasn't very likely. So at the end of the show we ran out of the stage door, rushed to the digs and went into the television room. The other guests were all sitting in front of the TV and, inevitably, they were watching the other channel.

"Umm… Excuse me everybody," said Warren, very politely. "I'm an actor appearing at the theatre this week and I'm actually in a play on the other side. It's just about to start and I'd love to watch it. Could we possibly switch over?"

They all just looked at him in silence for a moment, then turned away and continued watching their programme. It was just as if Warren hadn't spoken!

* * *

My other play that year was an interesting three-hander called *Don't Let Summer Come* at the Mermaid Theatre. Well, I say three-hander but there was a fourth character too, whom we'll get to in a minute.

I was a great admirer of the Mermaid because it had been founded just after the war by that excellent actor-director Bernard Miles. It was the City of London's only theatre and very much Bernard's baby. By the 1960s it was taking on all the newest theatre ideas, though maybe *Don't Let Summer Come* was too far out even for the most switched-on audiences. But it was a very clever psychological piece, I thought – the author was Terence Feely – and I was keen to do it.

My co-stars were Kenneth Griffith and Caroline Mortimer (daughter of John). At the beginning of the play, Caroline and I addressed the audience, asking for a volunteer to come up on stage. The seemingly reluctant gentleman who responded was, of course, a 'plant' – it was Kenneth. The play involved Caroline and me trying to drive this chap mad, to destroy him both mentally and physically. There was even a mocked-up elevator on stage that lit up to indicate the little man's descent to each new level of humiliation.

Caroline and I played a new character for all seven of these levels. At the end of each section we'd go behind a screen and come back as different characters. Our basic costume was a black leotard which we'd add to as necessary. As drum majorettes we added tassels, for intellectual actresses we put on great chunky sweaters, as nurses we had little hats and aprons, etc.

"The scene: a room," said the programme. "The time: now, perhaps." Which pretty much summed it all up, really. In fact, the set represented a sparsely furnished flat – just two chairs and a bed. It was all very obscure but it was the 1960s and I loved it. The audience seemed to read all sorts of bizarre messages into the play and that was exactly what was intended.

The play ended with Kenneth going completely mad. He had a speech about being swallowed up by tubes and he'd scream out his final line, "I'm going down the tubes!" At this point the lift door opened and out came this giant of a man. This was the weightlifter Dave Prowse, who'd later find fame as Frankenstein's Monster, the Green Cross Code Man and, of course, Darth Vader. Dave picked Kenneth up and carried him into the lift. Symbolically, this broken little man was being dragged down to Hell. We'd succeeded.

The play aroused all sorts of controversy. Quite unjustly, we were accused of 'lewdness'. It was claimed that Caroline and I were stripping on stage – which was utter nonsense, because, if anything, we just put more and more clothes *on*. Incredibly, the mere fact that we did our costume changes on stage – behind a screen! – gave the play a reputation.

It did no harm at the box-office, of course. In fact, I have an idea that Bernard himself fanned the flames. He was very clever where publicity was concerned.

During the run, Caroline and I received an anonymous letter – of the threatening variety. This crank was calling for the play to be taken off and for more wholesome fare to be presented instead. We even had a police escort for a time but it was all a storm in a teacup.

Never mind threatening letters and police escorts – our main problem was Kenneth Griffith. The man was a maniac, pure and simple. During rehearsals he'd insisted that we were all letter-perfect but during the run he took every opportunity to deviate from the text. He was a nightmare to work with from start to finish. He messed us around to an unbelievable degree. We never knew what he was going to do next, and not in a fun way – he was really quite destructive. I'd be trying to say a speech, for example, and he'd be goose-stepping round and round me, Nazi-style.

When Caroline and I told Bernard that Kenneth was sabotaging our performances, all he'd say was, "Yes, I know he is. But he's a force of nature, is Kenneth. Besides, you all have the same agent. I can't be seen to be treading on people's toes."

Kenneth was as peculiar off stage as on. He was an avid collector of two things – stamps and wives, and his private life was a complete mess as a result. He had three wives in various stages of divorce or separation, and was always getting messages from them at the stage door. In order to keep track, the doorman would mark them Number 1 Wife, Number 2 Wife, Number 3 Wife etc. On top of all that Kenneth was having an affair with a well-known female singer from the USA who was at the same time having an affair with an even more well-known singer – Dusty Springfield! He really was quite outrageous.

Eventually Bernard came up with what he presumably thought was a constructive suggestion. He hit upon Kenneth's big "I'm going down the tubes!" moment and said to me, "Where are you standing when he does that speech?"

"I'm standing at the back," I said.

"Well, when he does that speech tonight, just do a high kick."

"I can't do that!"

"Well, I can't *say* anything to him. That's the best solution I can come up with!"

I never did do that high kick. In fact, I remembered that during rehearsals Bernard had told us a little story about his very early career, when he'd succeeded in upstaging a fellow actor just by the subtlest of arm movements. So maybe Bernard was secretly relishing the anarchy of it all – and maybe that little anecdote had been a source of inspiration to our lunatic co-star!

Anyway, we finally got our own back on dear Kenneth. For the very last night, Caroline and I actually *rehearsed* what we were going to do to him. During the segment when he goose-stepped all round us we had to give him a bath. It was a dry bath; we never actually used water. But on that last night we gave him a real soaping. We were chucking water all over him and swabbing him down. Every time he stood up to say a speech we pirouetted round him, and whenever he tried to walk anywhere we tripped him up. It was very funny for everyone in the audience and even funnier for Caroline and me. Kenneth wasn't laughing much, though.

I have a feeling that the playwright was in that night – and he didn't really appreciate the shenanigans either. But it was wonderful to stitch Kenneth up after everything he'd put us through. He'd been such a disgrace throughout the run. The whole point of the play was to completely destroy his character. Well, on that last night we completely destroyed Kenneth Griffith.

* * *

During my Hollywood stint, I'd had a few American film offers but turned them all down because of my relationship with Bill Hitchcock. Bill was living with me in my Highgate flat by this time, but I still felt very insecure. In fact, all the time I was in America I was terrified that he would go back to his wife. The fact that I'd had an affair with a married man was against everything I believed in – yet he'd told me he was so dreadfully unhappy at home and that his wife didn't understand him, etc etc.

I know, I know. I was living through the whole 'cheating husband' cliché. But I believed him because I loved him.

Bill was also drinking very heavily – because, I thought, of his marital problems. In fact, I was always meeting him at the little pub just around the corner from Associated-Rediffusion. At the time, I thought he drank because he was unhappy. He didn't. He just drank because he drank.

All the TV directors drank copious amounts in those days. They weren't all drunks but they were all drinkers. They'd come out of that television building and head instinctively for the pub. No one thought any more about it, though for some it became a problem. For Bill it certainly became a problem.

So I married him.

I became Mrs Elizabeth Hitchcock on the 9th of January 1965. Bill and I were married at the Harrow Register Office and had only two friends as witnesses – our very best friends at that time, the composer Laurie Johnson and his wife Dot.

For our honeymoon we went on a two-week Mediterranean cruise on the Greek Line's QSS Arkadia. "Everything's wonderful," I told the *Daily Mirror*, "but I'll have to take a back seat to Diana Dors when we get back."

This was a joke, of course. Bill was about to start directing Diana in an *Avengers*-style TV series called *The Unusual Miss Mulberry*. Incidentally, it was one of Bill's saddest moments, years later, when he discovered that all the tapes of this series had been wiped. How some TV executive could imagine that a show starring Diana Dors had no historical value I'll never know.

A wonderful political drama called *When the Kissing Had to Stop*, plus loads of Bill's other work, had gone the same way. They'd all been shot on tape and were junked. So sad. Bill was heartbroken but there was nothing he could do about it.

* * *

When Bill and I got married we made an unofficial pact – we would never work together. It seemed sensible to get on with our own careers; that way we'd be able to go home to a normal married life. Though what *is* a normal life when you're both in the business? Bill was directing all the top ATV shows at the time and, not long after our honeymoon, I signed up for a play at the Royal Court Theatre in Sloane Square.

I'd had a call from my agent to say that there was a new play coming up called *Meals on Wheels*. It was written by Charles Wood and was to be directed by none other than John Osborne, author of *Look Back in Anger* and *The Entertainer*. I was told that Roy Kinnear, Frank Thornton and Lee Montague had already been cast, and I was thrilled – I liked every one of them.

We actors later discovered, of course, that we'd all been spun the same line – "such and such has already signed on" – when in fact such and such had done nothing of the sort. But it was a clever way of arousing our interest and I thought *Meals on Wheels* would be a fun piece of theatre to do.

The cast was the deciding factor because I wasn't too keen on doing more theatre at that time. I'd only been married a few months and the thought of spending all my evenings away from Bill wasn't very appealing. I read the play and – as usual with my theatre work in the 1960s – didn't understand a word of it! None of us did. There were lots of non-sequiturs and the whole thing seemed very odd. But it was booked in for a limited run of only three weeks, the cast was very good – and, besides, John Osborne was directing! How could I possibly turn it down?

When we started rehearsing at the Royal Court rehearsal rooms, which were above the pub next door, John Osborne seemed remote, to put it mildly. He was meant to be directing us but he did absolutely nothing. Admittedly, we were standing throughout the whole play, so there weren't many moves to be given, but he gave us no direction whatsoever. He barely said a word to us.

At one point I had to wear a bracelet with a balloon attached to it on a string. It was one of the very first helium balloons and, naturally, it would occasionally float up to the ceiling of the Royal Court! Anyway, it was at this moment that we all had to come out with random pieces of dialogue like: "I'm 24," "I'm 37," "I'm 92" and so on. For no reason that any of us actors could see. In fact, we all went down to the pub one day to try and work out what the hell the play was all about – and what John Osborne was really thinking. We never met the author, Charles Wood, and were completely mystified. We were also dreading the opening night.

Then, on the Saturday before we were due to open, John Osborne finally spoke. "I want you all to meet me outside the theatre," he said. He was with his wife, Penelope Gilliatt, and when a taxi came along we all bundled into it. It took us to the London Palladium, where Ken Dodd was playing. We thought it was just a nice treat prior to opening night and had a great time watching Ken Dodd doing his tickling stick stuff.

When we came out of the Palladium, John Osborne turned to us and said, "That's how I want you all to be."

With that he went off with his wife and we never saw him again!

The 'Friends of the Royal Court' were due in on the Monday, with the proper first night audience coming in on the Tuesday. Usually, the opening night with the Friends is very pleasant, as you'd expect. Well, this time it was a disaster. For our individual speeches we each had a strong spotlight on us, but when the light wasn't on me I could see the audience quite clearly. I saw loads of people just getting up out of their seats and walking out, and at the end of the play we had a slow hand-clap.

I thought to myself, "God almighty, if these are the 'Friends' of the theatre, what on earth is the paying audience going to be like?"

Anyway, this slow hand-clap went on and on. Some idiot in the wings brought the curtain down – fine – but then reeled it up again! It came down again – and then went up again with this slow hand-clap still going on. It went down a third time and when it started going up once more we all shouted, "Don't put the curtain up again!" Roy Kinnear actually grabbed hold of the tabs. They ripped about five feet with Roy still hanging on!

Naturally, we weren't looking forward to the first night proper, but we reasoned that an audience who'd paid for their tickets were far less likely to walk out than the 'Friends'. Oh, but how they walked out! Droves and droves of them. At the end we got another slow hand-clap, but not quite such a loud one this time as there were so few people left in the auditorium.

Anyway, the theatre's artistic director at the time was a young chap called Anthony Page. He came round afterwards and knocked on my dressing room door. It was traditional at the time to give actresses the Number One dressing room, and as I was the only woman in the cast mine was the first dressing room he came to.

"That was wonderful!" he cried.

"How can you say that was wonderful?" I asked incredulously. "They were all walking out!"

Then, after a slight pause, he came out with what, to me, has to be the classic line of all time.

"Yes," he said, "but their backs were electric!"

And with that he left. I then heard him knocking on all the other dressing room doors and saying the same thing to all the other members of the cast.

The next night I had another knock at my dressing room door, but this one was to give us notice! We were only booked to play for three weeks anyway, so to get notice on the third night was not good. We still had to keep plugging away for another ten days though, and because no one was willing to buy tickets the theatre was filled up with servicemen from the NAAFI.

To our amazement, these military types laughed a lot. There was a particular line of Roy's – "Clap hands if it comes out green!" – which was our cue to clap hands in unison. None of us ever understood what that meant. "Why did they laugh at that line?" puzzled Roy at the end – and then the penny dropped.

It turned out that it was a reference to VD – when a man had the clap his emissions would come out green. The play was full of obscure military gags like that, gags the actors and the West End audience didn't get but which the blokes from the NAAFI most certainly did. In fact, they laughed uproariously.

As I said, John Osborne was never seen again but I did receive a hand-written card from him when the dust had settled. It's dated the 10th of June 1965 and reads:

> Dear Liz
> I meant to come round and see you before the end of *MOW* but, unfortunately, I couldn't make it. I must thank you for being so wonderful in a difficult play and in difficult

circumstances. I do hope we do something again together one day. Good luck.
Love – John

Do something again one day? Well, well, well... I decided I wouldn't hold my breath.

* * *

Later in 1965 I went into Bernard Shaw's *Too True To Be Good* at the Garrick Theatre, which could well be my favourite West End assignment simply because it gave me the opportunity to work with the marvellous Alastair Sim. He was probably my favourite actor in the whole world and I was honoured to meet and work with him.

I took over the role of Nurse Sweetie from Dora Bryan, who was going off to do a film, and the company included lovely people like George Cole and T P McKenna. Most of my attention was focused on Alastair, however. I didn't have any major scenes with him but there were a lot of group scenes during which I always kept an eye on what he was doing. Whenever he wasn't talking, I'd watch him carefully as he listened to the person who *was* talking. He'd raise an eyebrow or incline his head very slightly – something lovely and subtle, and different, at every performance. Just watching a brilliant actor like Alastair Sim was like being given a masterclass in comic acting.

Of course, a new actor coming into an established production, albeit only for the last few months, can cause problems for other members of the cast. Though Dora and I are both actresses with a reputation for comedy, we're nevertheless vastly different in how we do things. She would have got a laugh on one line and I wouldn't get a laugh there; instead, I'd get a laugh on a line that she *hadn't* got a laugh on.

I rehearsed with the understudies so the first time I acted opposite George Cole was also the first time I performed the part in front of an audience. It must have been daunting for him, to say the least. In fact, he was completely thrown. We were getting lots of laughs that hadn't been there before, maybe because it was a sexy part and that was more my style than Dora's.

George apologised after we came off stage, saying, "I'm sorry I trod on that laugh, Liz, but we don't usually get a laugh there."

I wasn't bothered, though. It was one of the happiest experiences of my acting life.

* * *

Despite *Too True To Be Good*, I was put off theatre for quite a few years after my Royal Court experience and found that television became my staple diet instead. I did several very good shows in the 1960s – *No Hiding Place*, *Harry's Girls*, the Alfred Marks sitcom *Fire Crackers* and a play with Lee Montague called *A Pain in the Neck*. But I suppose my favourite is *The Avengers*. To this day I still get lots of fan mail about that show, so it obviously has great appeal even now.

It was October 1965 and for some reason Diana Rigg was unavailable for this episode, 'The Girl from Auntie' – most of it anyway. So the script was rejigged at the last minute and I was brought in as Georgie Price-Jones. Diana, of course, had worn some outrageous costumes as Emma Peel but I wanted to try a different approach.

"I play an ordinary girl caught up in unusual circumstances – which I handle unspectacularly," I told *TV Mirror*. "We discussed my wearing kinky clothes but I thought it would seem far too contrived."

So I was the new companion to Patrick Macnee's John Steed – for just that one episode. Patrick was very welcoming and considerate; he was an absolute gentleman. I'd worked with the director, Roy Ward Baker, before – he was always calm and collected, with no fuss made. He'd made epic feature films, so he just breezed through a television show. Not that he treated it with any less dedication. He was simply a very safe pair of hands.

We did it all very tongue in cheek, of course. I remember using all the Emma Peel throws in the fight sequence, then stopping mid-battle to consult a self defence book. It was great to be the female Avenger for that one episode and, on top of that, it was a very good part. In fact, it was very much a comic twist on the whole *Avengers* formula (which was pretty frothy and frivolous to start with), and of course that suited me down to the ground.

Another TV show I very much enjoyed was *Mickey Dunne*, which, though virtually forgotten today, was a really excellent BBC series. I remember doing a publicity session with some of the other girls in the show, including Jennie Linden and Judy Geeson. Dindsale Landen was the star as cockney wideboy Mickey Dunne – a sharp dresser who dined at all the best places but was nervous of women and couldn't really handle himself in a fight.

I appeared in the first episode as a drunken character called Maisie who was constantly lurching towards Mickey and saying, "You don't like me, do you?" This became something of a catchphrase. People who'd seen the show would regularly come up to me and say, "You don't like me, do you?"

Years later, when Dinsdale was suffering from cancer, I bumped into him on the Thames towpath near Putney Bridge. I stopped him and said, "You don't like me, do you?" We laughed so much and shared a few memories. He died soon afterwards.

* * *

Though I was turning down a lot of offers (including a Charlie Drake picture), I was still doing a few films from time to time.

In 1966 I was reunited with John and Roy Boulting on *The Family Way* and got to dance with John Mills. I also had a piece of lovely dialogue that sticks in my mind the same way as "Are them your own teeth?" from *I'm All Right Jack* does. Barry Foster was playing my husband and at one point I caught him boasting about what he'd like to do to Hywel Bennett's wife. "You'd do a job for him?" I said. "You? You couldn't do a job for our cat! Why, the milkman's been doing *your* bloody job for years!"

The year after that I did *Up the Junction* for director Peter Collinson. This one was based on a TV play by Nell Dunn. It was an earthy kitchen sink drama with Suzy Kendall playing a posh Chelsea girl who longs to live in the roughest part of Battersea.

I played Mrs McCarthy – my daughters were Maureen Lipman and Adrienne Posta – and I was delighted to be cast in the film. I felt it consolidated the route I was taking from blonde glamour girl to proper character actress. There I was, with dark roots and rollers in my hair. On location, the first time I walked down the street – hair in a mess, bags under my eyes, looking absolutely dreadful really – a stranger recognised me at once and called out "Here's Liz Fraser!"

Up the Junction opened in January 1968, by which time I'd taken the plunge and accepted another theatre job. The reason I did was because the script was so good. Peter Shaffer's double-bill of one-act plays, *The White Liars* and *Black Comedy*, starred James Bolam, Dorothy Reynolds and Ian McKellen. Ian, of course, has since become world-famous as Gandalf in the *Lord of the Rings* films. I still have a mug he gave me, with an 'L' on it.

The first play was a brilliant three-hander set in a seaside resort. The second – in which Robert Flemyng, Angela Scoular and I joined the three leads – was even better. I thought it was simply the funniest play I had ever done.

The really clever theatrical trick in *Black Comedy* was that the action started in the dark. The concept was that the actors had to play the opening scene as if they were lit – then there was a power cut and the stage was flooded with light. So the audience could see what was going on but we had to play it as though we were in the dark. It worked wonderfully well.

We opened in Brighton in February and then transferred to the Lyric Theatre on Shaftesbury Avenue. My role, Clea, was mistress to the Robert Flemyng character and had originally been played at the National Theatre by Maggie Smith and on Broadway by Geraldine Page. They were rather big boots to fill but I had a very nice notice from *The Listener*, which read:

> There are two good, easy parts for humorous girls in Peter Shaffer's fine farce. All that's needed for the dream-girl role is mature young stardom. Maggie Smith had it; in my view, Liz Fraser equals her.

The other dream-girl part, Carol, was played by Angela Scoular, who later married Leslie Phillips. She gave the sweetest ingenue performance. She simply sparkled. She was a delightful actress and delightful company. It was tragic to hear in April 2011 that she had taken her own life.

CHAPTER NINE

Elizabeth 200

In June 1968 came the dreadful news that Tony Hancock had committed suicide in Australia. I wept bitter tears for dear Tony. He was a wonderful talent and a fantastic human being, self-destructive yet utterly brilliant. A truly gifted funny man who never thought he was funny.

I'd last worked with him on *The Rebel* back in 1960, but we'd kept in touch over the years. We'd bump into each other at the odd premiere or film industry gathering.

Straight after making that film he'd had a tremendous success with his new BBC series, *Hancock*. Fans often say, "Well, Hancock was never as good without Sid." Yet if you ask them what their favourite episode is, they'll say 'The Radio Ham' or 'The Blood Donor' or 'The Lift'. And Sid wasn't in any of them. So, to a degree, Tony had been proved right in his 'go it alone' strategy. After that, though, I was well aware that things had gone badly wrong for him. For a start, he ditched his writers, Ray Galton and Alan Simpson, and that really was a bridge too far. While they went on to create *Steptoe and Son*, Tony's career just nose-dived.

Back when we were working together, Tony was always telling me that he'd never wanted to get married. He had, though, and Cicely, his formerly tee-total wife, went down the 'If you can't beat them, join them' route and became an alcoholic like him.

There was also a publicity lady who'd always loved him from afar. This was Freddie Ross. When Tony and Cicely divorced, he was in a really bad way and confided to me that, despite appearances, he really didn't want to marry Freddie either. But he was so hopelessly drunk at the time that he would have agreed to anything just to shut her up.

"Well, if she wants me, she can have me!" he told me.

I then had lunch with them on their wedding day in December 1965 and once again Tony told me that he hadn't wanted to marry her. We went back to Freddie's flat for the evening and Tony became horribly drunk. Tony was hosting *The Blackpool Show* for ATV at the time and it was in the middle of one of these live transmissions that Freddie attempted suicide – for the first time. The newspapers were up in arms, slamming Tony for not rushing down to see her. The publicity was horrendous.

As it turned out, their divorce was just going through when he headed off for Australia. But it had yet to become absolute when he died, so Freddie became the widow instead of the divorced wife. As for Tony, making the TV series *Hancock Down Under* must have seemed like the end of the line. His suicide note apparently read, "Things just seemed to go wrong too many times."

At least Tony managed to patch things up with Sid shortly before the end. When Sid had his first heart attack in 1967, slap bang in the middle of Tony's frantic marriage to Freddie, Tony made the effort to telephone Sid's wife, Valerie, and asked how his old mate was getting along. That took a lot of nerve on Tony's part. It was something I could never have imagined him doing, but he did.

* * *

Bill and I had moved away from Highgate by this time and were living in Hatch End. I'd also become a volunteer for the Samaritans, the charity set up by Chad Varah to support people who were contemplating suicide.

I'd gone along to a church in the City for an introductory session and I sat there with a lot of well-spoken ladies in big hats who presumably thought that talking to would-be suicides over the telephone would be a worthwhile addition to their charity work. The founder, Chad Varah himself, gave a talk about what volunteers were likely to come up against. I remember him slowly unwrapping a Kit Kat as he explained that we could expect to hear a lot of obscenities.

"You'll get sex calls," he warned us, "and you'll have to put up with words like 'fuck' and lots of other things that will probably shock many of you."

Well, needless to say, there weren't many of those well-spoken ladies left when I turned up for the second session.

I stayed with the Samaritans for 13 years altogether. We all had identification numbers and mine was 'Elizabeth 200'. Callers would phone the main switchboard and ask for 'Elizabeth 200', then I'd phone them back; they never learned your personal number. I'd work the early morning shift from 6.00 am until 9.00 am two days a week.

And it turned out Chad Varah had been right about the sex calls. I'd often get calls from public telephone boxes, and these anonymous gentlemen would actually be wanking as they talked to me! If asked I'd always tell them that I was wearing red knickers! The good thing about this, to my mind, was that if they were phoning me then at least they weren't bothering some other poor woman, because in those days there were an awful lot of heavy-breathers about.

I had several very sad cases come to me. One of the women I'd befriended, a woman with two children, did actually commit suicide while I was away on a cruise for three weeks. She put her head in a gas oven. We'd been getting really friendly and I was dreadfully shocked. I was very dedicated to the work so I really felt that I'd let her down. It was very upsetting.

Another lady, I remember, had a pathological hatred of other women; she wouldn't even allow her husband to watch women on television. I'd also talk to wife-swappers. Some of these people actually lived just around the corner from me and I couldn't help smiling whenever I walked past their houses. In the end, they swapped full time and went off with each other's partners.

Actually, I went too far in some cases. One woman told me that I was the first Samaritans person she'd spoken to and that she was very upset because her husband was having an affair. The other woman was a nudist and he'd go off every weekend to see her. Though we weren't supposed to give direct advice, I told her that, when he came back from his next nudist weekend, she should call her husband's bluff and parade around the house with no clothes on! It was only a joke but I was immediately hauled in and quizzed about it. "What on earth have you been telling this lady?" etc etc. Apparently she'd done what I said, then phoned up while I wasn't in and asked what should she do next?

All this was a bit ironic because my own domestic life was anything but secure at this time. Not only was Bill drinking more and more, he'd also returned to his old womanising ways. I'd been told time and time again that he'd never change, but I'd convinced myself that I was 'the one'. As I found out later, however, he'd gone back to his usual pattern from virtually the minute we were married.

He had a string of affairs, one with his secretary at ATV, then another with his PA at London Weekend Television, and yet another with a production assistant in Leeds. I first found out about Bill's behaviour when he was having an affair with his secretary at Yorkshire Television. I was furious. In fact, I put all his stuff in some suitcases and threw them out of the house. He was very good indeed at talking me round, though, so those suitcases were on and off that pavement many times during our nine-year marriage.

The comedy writer Sid Colin, who was a very good friend of mine, said to me one time, "But didn't *you* have an affair with him while he was married? So what did you expect? You knew what he was like when you married him!"

That was true. But, of course, you never listen.

* * *

As well as working for the Samaritans, I was also devoting much of my time – as I still do – to another charitable foundation, the Variety Club of Great Britain. I first became involved in the early 1960s, and in 1975 received the club's Silver Heart award at the London Hilton, with an International Presidential Citation following in the 1980s.

Back in the 1960s and '70s, the Variety Club attracted all the biggest stars. I particularly enjoyed getting to know the sporting personalities. I met Sir Alf Ramsey and Bernie Ecclestone on several occasions, but it was the boxers that I really liked.

I was heavily involved with the youth clubs, which, at that time, had their own boxing rings. The various boys' clubs would compete against each other, with the finals being held in a posh hotel somewhere. As a result of my involvement, I became a big boxing fan and saw some amazing fights. For example, I vividly remember Bill and I seeing the Henry Cooper versus Cassius Clay fight in June 1963. Henry ultimately lost but I saw him deliver that famous left hook in the final seconds of the fourth round. I subsequently saw him fight Joe Bugner and got to see him in person at the various Variety Club events.

I knew all the boxers and would always get a kiss on the cheek from them. The cockney middleweight Terry Downes was one of my favourites. He was known as the Paddington Express but was really charming outside the ring.

He pulled me aside one time and said, "'Ere, Liz, d'you know what? Someone came up to me the other day and asked for me autograph. I signed it and this bloke said 'But I can't read it!' And I said, 'Well, if I could write I wouldn't be a bleeding boxer, would I?'"

Another person I got to know very well through the Variety Club was Sir James Carreras, the head of Hammer Films. I'd made *Watch It, Sailor!* for Hammer but longed to be in one of their Dracula films – the fangs, the blood and Christopher Lee. It wasn't to be, but I remained friendly with James and would often be invited to his office in Wardour Street.

In the corridors at Hammer House there were lots of lurid posters on display, advertising all their horrific Frankenstein and Dracula films. One day my attention was drawn to one of these posters and I said, "I've not seen that one. I haven't even heard of it."

"No, you wouldn't have," he replied. "We haven't made it yet. That's the way we do things here."

"What do you mean?" I asked.

"Well, we commission a poster and then we get financial backing for the film by showing the poster to the backers."

I thought this was a brilliant idea. The poster that had caught my eye was for a film that was to be set in a little Cornish village. I remembered that there'd been another film a few years before, produced by a rival company, called *The Village of the Damned*. This gave me an idea. I wanted to write a screenplay so I started work on a storyline about a mysterious village.

It was all rather vague. A man is looking out of a window and he sees a woman walking towards him ... Another man comes along ... Then some other people join them ... They're all in a village where a murder has taken place ... And more murders follow. The village has a publican, naturally, and he has a wife ... And a gardener...

After writing about ten pages of this I realised that I hadn't given names to any of the characters. I'd just been saying 'he' or 'she' and even I couldn't remember which 'he' or 'she' I was talking about at any given time. So that was that. I lost interest and I didn't write any more.

I was very proud of it at first, though, so I said to Sir James, "I'm doing a film for you. I'm writing it now. I have a title, too – *The Village of Death*."

"Well," he cried. "That would make a wonderful poster!"

That was praise enough. To be a potential poster on the walls of the House of Hammer...

Away from Wardour Street, Sir James often invited me to be his guest at various Variety Club events. One of these was at the Grand Hotel in Bristol.

The Variety Club is divided into what are called 'tents'. We in London were Tent 36 and now they were going to open a new south-western tent in Bristol. The Bristol tent was short-lived, as it turned out, but the opening was a grand affair. Jimmy Edwards, Linda Hayden and myself were the showbusiness guests and we were surrounded on all sides by wealthy stockbrokers and industrialists.

At dinner, Sir James was seated on my left, and there was a big catalogue in front of him listing all the wines that were due to be auctioned that evening.

"Liz," he said, "you can have whichever case of wine you want!"

I knew absolutely nothing about wines so I turned to the man on my right, who just happened to be the head of Berni Inns, and asked him which wine Sir James should bid for. He pointed out the best one; it was number 47 on the list and was a case of vintage Château Lafite. I don't recall the year but he assured me it was the best vintage possible and by far the best case in the auction. It also turned out to be the most expensive. Sir James bought it for me and the case was duly delivered to my home.

Bill and I both liked wine. All I knew about it, though, was that it should be laid down on slats, which I did. After a week or so, we opened one of the bottles and it tasted absolutely awful. Neither of us liked it and I decided it must have been a bad bottle. So we opened another one and that was awful too. Eventually I used one of the other bottles for cooking and it spoiled the meal! I came to the conclusion that the whole case was bad, so I threw it away.

How naïve can you get? I only discovered what a fool I'd been years later when I was watching an episode of *Columbo* on television. Donald Pleasence was the murderer; he'd killed his brother and to establish an alibi he'd stored his victim in the wine cellar. He'd altered the temperature in order to preserve the body, making it look as if his brother had died a day or so later than he actually did. But the weather had turned unexpectedly hot in the meantime and Columbo trapped him by noticing that the wine had been heated and thereby ruined.

Well, not only did I realise that Donald Pleasence was going to be banged up for murdering his poor brother but I also realised that through sheer stupidity I had murdered 12 bottles of the most expensive wine in the world. When I'd put the wine down on slats, the slats I'd chosen were the ones in the immersion heater! So every day before I opened that first bottle, this vintage Château Lafite had been boiled and cooled and boiled and cooled...

It's now worth something like a thousand pounds a bottle.

* * *

I may not have cared for vintage wine properly, but I lavished a lot of affection on two of my absolute passions – cars and dogs.

I've always loved cars, and my first one – the Ford Anglia I'd got from Lansing Bagnall in 1959 – didn't last long before I traded it in for an MGB. Then I had a Lotus 2+2 for 11 years, then another Lotus for a further seven. Then there was a Mazda RX7 and, after that, a Honda Prelude with four-wheel steer. (Not made these days.) I loved that car, and every three years I'd change its colour. After 27 years it finally gave up the ghost. All its innards had been replaced at one time or another and I thought it would last forever. But nothing ever does and it was finally towed away, with me watching it until it was out of sight.

More recently I ordered an Alfa Romeo but common sense finally kicked in; I was only making short journeys so I now run the 50th anniversary edition of a Mini Cooper S, named Camden – not by me, I hasten to add, by BMW. I've been driving for 50-odd years now and have never had an accident.

After my childhood experiences at the dog tracks, greyhounds continued to play a big role in my life. Through the Variety Club I was invited to various charity meets, usually at the tracks at Hackney and Hendon. Pretty much throughout the 1960s I went to the track every Saturday morning, watching all the races – eight of them, with six dogs per race – over a full English breakfast. The stadiums were packed in those days. I loved the atmosphere and knew all the people there. Oddly enough, it was at one of these events that I first met Leslie Phillips.

Anyway, my love of greyhounds led to me actually investing in some. Arthur Holden, the director at Hackney and Hendon, took me to an auction of Irish puppies and I found it fascinating to compare all the bid prices. One particular litter attracted very high sums, but I noticed there was one pup left that seemed to be going cheaply. I felt the other bidders had bought quite enough by this time, so up went my hand and down came the hammer. Quinella Queen was mine!

"What have you done?" gasped Arthur. "Are you mad? You'll have to have a license, and a trainer… You'll just lose money! And anyway, you've bought the runt of the litter!"

None of this bothered me. Every Sunday I'd go along to visit Quinella Queen at Hackney Stadium, taking bags of Maltesers and little bits of cooked chicken. After every race I'd be there to cuddle her; she nearly always lost but I'd make a huge fuss of her.

When I was away on holiday she was killed on the track. The tracks were grass in those days – very slippery – and she'd collided with the fence, breaking her neck. Not knowing what had happened I went to visit her at the track as usual and couldn't find her. A horrified trainer, who assumed I'd been told already, had to break it to me that she'd been put down. I cried and cried and decided I could never get that close to one of my greyhounds ever again.

Even so, I did eventually buy another two dogs, County Printer and Lizzie Hook's Kid. They weren't great winners but they were a source of huge interest to me and both eventually retired to nice homes. Someone once asked me, incidentally, if Lizzie Hook's Kid was actually me and I said "No." But of course it was, Hook having been my mother's maiden name.

My passion for greyhounds continues to this day. They've given me a lot of pleasure throughout my life and, as a little thank you, I've left money to the Greyhound Rescue Charity in my will.

It was the greyhounds that got me involved in stocks and shares. At a Variety Club luncheon I'd found myself sitting next to a top city broker, who gave me his card just in case I ever felt like trying my hand at the Stock Market. The next weekend I started a race on behalf of the Territorial Army. This was at the request of one of the Hackney and Hendon directors, who advised me to buy shares in the company as soon as I could.

"OK," I thought. I phoned the broker and bought £100 of shares at two-and-a-half pence each. The track was sold and became the Brent Cross Shopping Centre; thankfully, all the greyhounds were given new homes. The shares shot up and I sold them for over £2 each. I reinvested the money and that was beginning of my years of playing the Stock Market.

* * *

After Janie the retired greyhound back at Harper Road in the 1930s, the family had progressed to an Alsatian and, later, two Cocker Spaniels.

Then in the mid-1960s a friend of mine was going off to look at a litter of Basset Hounds and invited me along. My friend's contact wasn't a proper breeder but, because her Basset, Diamond Lil, had mated, she was keen to get rid of the pups. I saw this little lemon-and-white puppy and fell in love with Bassets on the spot. They are the most adorable dogs.

Bill and I had yet to move to Hatch End at this point; we were still in our ground-floor flat in Highgate and the block we were in didn't allow dogs. But I loved this tiny pup so much that I told the owner of the block that it was the runt of the litter and, in theory, would stay very small. Eventually he relented and I came home with Busby Basset. Bill would often take him to the pub with him. I didn't know it then, but a dog is an excellent means of attracting women!

Subsequently, Busby Basset would tour with me all round the country for years and years. Every one of my cars had to be big enough to house a Basset in the back and we drove long distances together. I was forever getting into trouble at digs because of my five-foot Basset. "It's just a small dog," I'd say on the phone when booking my stay.

Busby Basset became an important part of my life. He'd even watch me play bridge; he was very intelligent! My association with Busby – and his successors Banjo, Bracken and now Brodie – led to a lovely friendship with Alex Graham, creator of the cartoon character Fred Basset, who drew lots of original cartoons for me. It also led to my taking over Alex's post as co-chairman of the Yorkshire, Lancashire and Cheshire Club for Basset Hounds.

I still write regularly for their newsletters and have done so for a long time now. All the funds go to the Basset Hound rescue schemes, which I have also remembered in my will.

* * *

Unfortunately, dogs had to be my only companions. I had very much wanted to have children but found that I wasn't able to conceive. I had numerous tests but the doctors couldn't find anything wrong. I'd see women with lots of children and wonder how on earth they managed it.

I wanted to adopt a child instead, but Bill already had children from his first marriage and didn't want to look after a child that wasn't his own. Many years later I had to have a hysterectomy, so there'd obviously been a fault there all the time. But it was hurtful when people remarked, "Oh, so you didn't want children then?"

What could I say? I just had Bassets.

CHAPTER TEN

Losing Bill

As the 1970s came along I was still doing plenty of television. I remember there was an episode of *Randall and Hopkirk (Deceased)* – the one where I was reunited with my first boyfriend, Graham Armitage – and later another ITC show, *Jason King* with Peter Wyngarde. And, having worked with all the comedy greats of a previous generation, I started on a whole new one by guest-starring in one of the first episodes of *The Goodies* – namely, Tim Brooke-Taylor, Graeme Garden and Bill Oddie. They were all quite mad, of course. The story involved me running a strip club catering exclusively to women, so instead of bunny girls we had bunny boys.

The cast of *Dad's Army* were a little bit older than *The Goodies*. When the film version was made in 1970, I was asked to play Mrs Pike, mother of Ian Lavender's gormless Private Pike. With the exception of Ian, all the men in *Dad's Army*, from Arthur Lowe down, had had years and years of experience. John Le Mesurier, in particular, had made loads of films. Film producers always want film people so, for this little part of Ian Lavender's mum, they wanted a film actress and called me in. I reasoned that the same thing had happened to me when the film version of *Whack-O!* was being cast ten years earlier. It's swings and roundabouts in this business. I wanted to do the *Dad's Army* film as I thought it would be great fun – which it was.

Oddly enough, just before the film came out in 1971 I recorded a radio pilot for *Parsley Sidings*, which had Arthur Lowe and Ian

Lavender as father and son, with Bill Pertwee popping in from time to time too. It was a lovely little comedy set in a tiny railway station, and subsequently we did two series of it.

One of my favourite performances was in a TV version of the Terence Rattigan play *Man and Boy*, starring opposite Telly Savalas and Gayle Hunnicutt. It was a great thrill to work with Telly, the future lollipop man, and he was brilliant in it; the play was excellent too.

I also did a pilot show called *These Two Fellas* with Frank Carson and Duggie Brown. Both of them had become well-known in *The Comedians*, which was produced by Johnny Hamp. He produced *These Two Fellas* as well, and was constantly telling Frank that he mustn't swear. But Frank said "bloody" this and "bloody" that virtually every other word. Unsurprisingly, no series followed and even the pilot was never broadcast.

* * *

My most enjoyable job at this time was a lovely BBC documentary for *The World About Us*. In this I 'played' myself and was investigating underground London, which meant things could get very smelly indeed. The major plus point was that my co-host was Captain Sir Ranulph Twisleton-Wykeham-Fiennes – or plain Ranulph Fiennes as he is now known.

Even then he was one of the best-known of all British explorers; indeed, he was preparing to go up the Canadian rapids the wrong way and was spending lots of his time trying to get sponsorship for this latest expedition. So, not a bad sort to explore subterranean London with.

For several weeks we literally spent all our time underground together. We went down a manhole beside the Serpentine sewers, travelled across the area beneath Hyde Park, and emerged, smelling a bit, outside Harvey Nichols in Knightsbridge. We were down there for days, wading through tunnels, encountering rats and gasping in amazement at some absolutely beautiful sewage works. The designs down there were breathtaking. Though at one point I would've welcomed my breath being taking away for real – when a whole load of sewage suddenly tumbled out of a side tunnel. Our escort and sewage expert calmly said, "Oh, that'll be from Lord So and So's place..."

Ran and I even danced down there – and in our waders to boot! I must say I've never had a more memorable dance than that one. We then emerged, smiling and laughing, from the manholes next to Eros in Piccadilly Circus.

We also visited an underground crypt and saw ancient skeletal remains at Brompton Cemetery. We went to Winston Churchill's War Rooms in the days when the general public weren't allowed to see them. We travelled on the little self-driving train that ran through the tunnels delivering the post. We visited a now disused tube station near London Bridge, which had been packed with people during the Blitz and still housed poignant mementoes. And we visited St Catherine's Dock near Tower Bridge, which retained the dungeons where prisoners were kept before being transported to Australia. The crimes they had committed were so minor – like stealing sheep. We saw the letters to loved ones that they'd left behind, and they were so moving. I read one aloud for the cameras – me being the actress and Ran being just an explorer!

I can honestly say that it was one of the most interesting and enjoyable jobs I've ever done. Ran was a delightful fellow, though I refused to go in a rowing boat with him across St Catherine's Dock. He may have been Britain's greatest explorer but, because I couldn't swim, I declined. All in all it was a great experience, and to my great delight I re-encountered Ran in March 2011 – a full 40 years later – at the Hurlingham Club, where he was giving a lecture and signing books. We met early for tea and had an enjoyable hour or two reliving our old adventures.

His own adventures in the intervening years, as I learned in the lecture, had been quite extraordinary; among other things, he'd lost a few more toes to frostbite. Signing his book, he wrote, "With happy memories of our sewer-dancing in 1971." I treasure it.

* * *

In 1972 Bill and I broke our longstanding pact about never working together. At the last minute he cast me as a sexy but over-the-hill air stewardess in the Rodney Bewes sitcom *Albert!* And later that year we did it again, this time for *Turnbull's Finest Half-Hour*, a six-part comedy series starring Michael Bates.

In the early 1970s Bill really was at his peak as a director of light entertainment television, working extensively for ATV and Yorkshire TV. He'd produced specials for Shirley Bassey and Tom Jones and had brought Ken Dodd to television with *Funny You Should Say That*. The shows they did together were the nearest anybody ever got to capturing the Dodd magic on screen.

Bill had also directed my old friends Sid James and Kenneth Connor in the television comedy *All This – And Christmas Too!* And as director of *Sez Les*, he'd brought Les Dawson and Roy Barraclough together in their famous characters of Cissie and Ada. This was simply because he'd seen them camping about together in the canteen during breaks in filming and had said, "We'll use that!"

For my part, I'd settled down to a domestic routine. The house in Hatch End was detached with a 160-foot garden, at the end of which we had a little orchard. I used to so enjoy picking my own fruit. (The birds had the cherries.) And both Bill and I loved a game of golf. He was a member of the Grim's Dyke Golf Club in Harrow Weald and I was a member at Mill Hill. I was still turning down stage work because I preferred to be at home with Bill in the evenings.

Bill was at his busiest and was also drinking a lot. He would be able to get drunk at work and still control a show, but at home he was drinking more and more. And of course the affairs continued unabated. In fact, one day I came home to a find a long dark hair on our pillow. He'd obviously brought his latest girlfriend back to our house – and bed.

I decided to go away for three weeks to give him time to extricate himself from this latest affair, and also because I needed time to think things through. I stayed with friends in Los Angeles. I was very close to leaving him because I simply couldn't stand it any longer. I told him that if he hadn't ended the relationship by the time I came back I would start divorce proceedings.

Before I made the return journey I'd been promised by Bill that the affair with the girl in Leeds was indeed over. He'd even arranged a holiday for the two of us so we could start afresh; it was to be a one-week golfing holiday followed by another week of just relaxing in the sun somewhere. I knew then that everything would be different.

On the very day I returned home, Bill died. He was just 41 years of age.

It was February 1974. I'd come home armed with several gifts for him – a cashmere cardigan and a crocodile card-holder, plus bottles of Aramis and Remy Martin. After he'd opened them all I went off to make coffee. I returned to the lounge to find Bill lying on the floor. I thought it was a joke at first and tried to make him get up. But after a few moments I realised something was seriously wrong. There was blood frothing from his lips. This was no joke.

I tried to lift him up. He was quite a big man and I couldn't manage it. At that moment my mind just blanked out. Some things you just remove from your memory because they're too painful to remember. I can't remember phoning for an ambulance. I can't remember Bill being taken to Mount Vernon Hospital. I can't remember phoning up two friends who lived nearby, and who were now by my side.

The first thing I *can* remember is the surgeon saying, "I'm very sorry, Mrs Hitchcock, but we haven't been able to resuscitate him."

I had to phone his ex-wife and tell her. I phoned the girl in Leeds who'd been his current girlfriend to let her know, too. I phoned

Dickie Henderson, who was Bill's very best friend and who was very helpful to me, organising the funeral and other things.

Later, the coroner told me that Bill had had very high blood pressure, so of course I thought that his death was my fault. I should never have gone away for those three weeks. I should never have given him such a hard time about the girl in Leeds. I should never have put him under such an awful lot of pressure. But the coroner assured me that the high blood pressure had built up over quite a long period of time and just at that moment it had bypassed the heart and flooded the lungs. He said that there was nothing to blame myself for; if it hadn't happened that day, he said, then it would have happened within the month anyway.

Women, cigarettes and vodka had taken their toll.

* * *

Almost as soon as Bill died, my agent, Richard Stone, rang up and said, "Look, Liz. Would you like to get away? I can get you into this play *Move Over Mrs Markham*. It's going to be a five-month season at the end of the pier in Bournemouth. Maurice Stewart is directing for John Gale Productions. Do you think that would be a good thing for you?"

Well, work concentrates the mind. So I immediately said, "Yes, I think that's a good idea."

I didn't want to be at home, alone, brooding over Bill's death. The play was due to co-star the lovely Millicent Martin, MacDonald Hobley, Doris Hare and Edwin Richfield. It seemed like the perfect escape route, and it was a very funny play, so I agreed to do it.

But there was something else I needed to attend to. I'd found a lump on my tummy and my GP had arranged an appointment for me at Northwick Park Hospital. By this time I'd started rehearsals for *Move Over Mrs Markham* so I asked the director for the Thursday afternoon off. As it turned out, I was kept in at the hospital because I needed a hysterectomy.

So, not only was I bereaved but I was now in the early stages of recovering from a major operation too, which was depressing in itself. The growth had apparently been equivalent in size to a six-month pregnancy.

My agent visited me in the hospital and said he'd try to get some alternative work for me as soon as I recovered.

"What do you mean?" I asked him. "I've still got *Move Over Mrs Markham*."

"Well, you can't do that," he replied.

"But I've been rehearsing! Why on earth can't I do it?"

"My dear Liz," said Richard. "It doesn't matter if you've been rehearsing. You've just had a hysterectomy. You can't go on with the play. They're casting Lynda Baron in your place."

"But that's not fair!" I fumed.

"Liz," Richard replied, "don't be ridiculous. My wife Sarah had a hysterectomy and she still hasn't recovered after six months."

"Well," I persisted, "what does my contract say?"

It turned out that there was a specific deadline after which an artiste would lose their role – and it was still a week away. So I discharged myself from the hospital, signing a paper on the way out to confirm that I took full responsibility for my actions. I had somebody drive my Lotus to Bournemouth and got someone else to take me and my luggage to the cottage I'd booked for the season. I could barely walk but I somehow got to the end of the pier and presented myself at the theatre.

With the exception of Millie Martin everyone was absolutely horrified. The producers had the choice of either keeping me on contractually or sticking with Lynda Baron, who at the time had only signed a short-term contract. Because I'd presented myself, they'd have had to pay me for the entire five months anyway, even if they didn't use me. So Lynda had to go.

Every time we rehearsed, Doris Hare would say, "Well, we didn't do it like that when Lynda was playing the part!"

Millie Martin would always come to my aid and say, "Well, it was Liz's part in the first place!"

Just to prove I wasn't a complete idiot, I got myself along to Poole Hospital where Jeremy Lee-Potter (husband of the journalist Lynda Lee-Potter) was the resident specialist. I'd been in great pain during the rehearsals but he cauterised me to stop the bleeding and I soldiered on. It was very tough but Millie was so supportive and, somehow, I got through it.

During the run, Jeremy would take me into the ward where all the women who had had hysterectomies were lying in bed and he'd say, "Look! Look what you could all do! She's just had one and she's all right."

By the end of the five months in Bournemouth I was in pretty good shape, having played eight shows a week and not missed a single performance. I'd been living in a lovely little cottage and the whole experience was the perfect tonic. Call it courage if you like. I call it obstinacy. I just refused to give up that part and it was definitely one of the best decisions of my life – I'm convinced it helped me through the pain.

During the run I couldn't face collecting my weekly widow's pension. But it was mounting up so at the end of the season I took the book into the Post Office. It was now a large-ish sum in £5 notes. "Your lucky day!" said the teller.

* * *

Busby Basset was certainly very helpful to me during the Bournemouth ordeal and, what's more, he became a star attraction!

It was a lovely summer season that year. Mike Yarwood was there, plus Roy Hudd and Lulu; even Cannon and Ball, who weren't yet famous on television. All these people, together with Millie Martin, were due to take part in a special midnight matinée, and I too was asked to appear.

"What can I do though?" I asked Roy.

"Well, you could do a dog act," he replied.

"How can I do a dog act?"

"Well, you've got the dog, haven't you?"

"Yes, thank you, Roy," I groaned. "But he can't *do* anything!"

"That's the joke."

He told me about this American guy who did a dog act with a dog that didn't do a single thing; they'd become quite famous, apparently. "Yes," I thought. "I could do that with Busby." So the stage was set with just a tall stepladder and a bucket on top of it, plus a large ball and a trolley. I was dressed in a sparkling leotard and came on with Busby Basset in tow. To a round of applause I picked him up and placed him on the trolley.

"This is Shirley Basset," I cried. "We have a veterinary surgeon in the wings just in case there's a serious accident. So let the drums roll." The dog looked at the audience. Nothing. "Drums again, please!" Nothing. "Sorry," I said. "He needs a round of applause before he performs this dangerous act."

The audience clapped and cheered but as the clapping died down I picked up the dog and said, "If you think he's going to do his act just for that – you're bloody wrong!"

I then wheeled him off. And that was our dog act. Busby was the star of the show.

Sadly, I had to have him put down in 1976, when he became very ill. After that, nearly two years went by before I was ready to replace him.

I was on tour, as usual, and went along to a dog show in Cardiff. I'd actually pre-ordered a new puppy from a breeder who had been recommended to me, a Mrs Rowett-Johns. Well, I sat at the ringside and noticed to my horror that the balls of all her male dogs were colossal and swung to and fro as they trotted around the ring. I turned to the lady sitting next to me.

"Are all her dogs like that?" I whispered.

"Oh yes," she replied. "Mrs Rowett-Johns is well known for her untidy testicles!"

So I cancelled my order and selected a different Basset from the same show. Thankfully, this one had very tidy balls indeed.

* * *

Maurice Stewart, director of *Move Over Mrs Markham*, also directed me in the Charles Dyer play *Rattle of a Simple Man*, which I toured in several times. In fact, I had three leading men – Frank Marlborough, Hugh Lloyd and John Junkin. I was playing the prostitute role originated on stage by Sheila Hancock and then played on film by Diane Cilento, and I loved it. It was a good dramatic part for me and I thoroughly enjoyed it.

I loved live audiences because I knew how to handle them. I always made sure to be completely fresh for each performance. I never said a line exactly the same way because, when you're doing the same show night after night, the rot can set in very quickly and your performance can seem mechanical to an audience. That's the kiss of death for theatre, so I'd think through my performances each and every time.

There was a memorable matinée performance of *Rattle of a Simple Man* in Bath. It was pouring with rain that day, and on top of that there was plenty of thunder and lightning. The theatre manager came up to us and explained that because the weather was so dreadful we only had five punters out front. He pointed out that it was theatre policy to cancel a show if there were fewer than 15 people in the auditorium. But he left it up to us as to whether we went on or not.

Well, I certainly wasn't about to dictate to the rest of the cast but I said, "If we were performing before the Queen there'd only be about five people watching anyway. So why don't we pretend that it's the Queen and the Duke of Edinburgh and a couple of other dignitaries out there, and do the show as if it were a Royal Command Performance?"

So on we all went. The manager put all five audience members in one row, about three rows back, and it was probably the best performance we ever gave. The audience thanked us personally afterwards. They'd paid and deserved to see us at our best.

The *Rattle of a Simple Man* tours gave rise to some memorable encounters. One was with the madcap young comic Freddie Starr, and it was a trial to say the least. I'd first met him at some charity do and we'd become fairly friendly; he'd pop in to see me in Hatch End and our chats were always pretty crazy. Nothing, however, could prepare me for our encounter when I was playing *Rattle of a Simple Man* in Blackpool.

I was just about to step into a café one day when I saw him across the street. I didn't stop to chat because we were playing Blackpool for three weeks and I knew I'd be seeing him at some point. Freddie must have spotted me, though, because he came into the café and sat down next to me just as I was tucking into my jacket potato. We greeted each other with some warmth and he said, "Where are you going now?"

"I'm going to finish my lunch," I spluttered, "and then I'm off to play golf."

"Where are you going to play golf?" he enquired.

I explained that I'd booked up at Royal Lytham & St Annes to play a round of golf with a fellow actor from the show. I'd reserved this session weeks and weeks in advance because this was the champion's golf course and it was a rare treat to play a round on it. Like me, my fellow actor, Geoffrey Collins, was a golf fanatic.

"Oh well," said Freddie, "I'm doing nothing. I'll come with you."

"Oh no, you won't!" I said.

He was so mad and so persistent that I ended up fleeing to my car while he sprinted to his. It was a very expensive car, a Rolls-Royce I expect, with FREDDIE 1 on the number plate. I raced off, hotly pursued by Mr Starr. I was a better driver than him but I still couldn't shake him off. Indeed, he arrived just behind me at the golf club.

Geoffrey, of course, was as horrified as I was.

"Why have you brought *him*?" he said.

"I didn't *want* him to come," I replied.

But by this time Freddie was standing next to us, grinning from ear to ear.

"We don't want you here, Freddie!" I bellowed.

"It's all right," he said. "I'm just going to walk round with you."

So Geoffrey and I took out our clubs and our tickets in order to start our long-awaited game on this famous golf course.

Well, Freddie Starr was with us every step of the way, keeping up all his usual inane banter. First he started to take out clubs and take pot shots. This you were definitely not allowed to do and I kept telling him so. By the third tee he'd removed his jacket and shirt. He then started to take off his trousers! So it was no surprise to Geoffrey and I when we were confronted on the fourth tee by the Secretary of the Royal Lytham & St Annes Golf Club and asked to leave. Our explanation that this lunatic wasn't actually with us fell on deaf ears. We were escorted off the green and that was that.

To be a golfer and have the chance to play on such a course is a rare honour. It was a big deal to me. And there was Freddie Starr doing everything he could to ruin it. I could have killed him. To make matters worse, the groundsmen had put some strange kind of fertiliser on the green and it eroded my beautiful new putter. It really was a disastrous day and I've never forgotten it.

So, a word of warning. If you're ever lucky enough to play at Royal Lytham & St Annes Golf Club, make sure you don't take Freddie Starr along!

* * *

My last go at *Rattle of a Simple Man* was with John Junkin. John was an excellent scriptwriter who also enjoyed acting, and he was marvellous in the play. I'd join him for drinks at Gerry's on Shaftesbury Avenue and we became good friends.

Gerry's was a popular showbusiness rendezvous and it was there, incidentally, that I met Jeffrey Bernard – who, when he wasn't drinking or making a bet, would ask me out, without success. He was too 'rich' for my blood. His life was later made into a play, *Jeffrey Bernard is Unwell*, starring Peter O'Toole. I saw it and thought it was brilliant, and also very evocative.

Anyway, the week before we started our tour together, John and I were drinking in Gerry's when I caught sight of a very attractive man. Sitting at the bar was a black-clad stranger sipping a soft drink. He said to me, "I wasn't expecting you until January." As it was September at the time, I thought, "What a line!"

This was Bill Mitchell. His wondrously deep voice was heard by millions on numerous TV commercials. I was bewitched by this hunk and forgot all about poor John. In fact, John left me behind with Bill but not before offering a dire warning.

"I should go careful there if I were you," he said.

This advice I ignored.

I was absolutely captivated by Bill Mitchell. We talked and talked and at three in the morning wandered around Covent Garden hand in hand. I'd seen this kind of thing in films; someone should have been selling violets somewhere! Then I took this treasure home for the weekend.

The play was due to open in Ayr on the Monday. Well, Bill followed me there, then to Torquay and goodness knows where else. I was smitten. When he wasn't around I'd rush back to my digs in the hope that the Pan Am commercial would come on. His deep voice saying "Fly Pan Am" would come out of the telly and send shivers down my spine.

He always wore black and never drank. Great! But, of course, there was a catch in all this. I soon discovered that my Adonis didn't drink because he was going through a dry spell under instructions from an acupuncturist. It turned out that this gorgeous hunk, whose black clothes were now hanging in my wardrobe, had been a mirage. Over night I found myself lumbered with a boring, pot-smoking, wine-guzzling slob who spent all his nights propping up bars in Soho, as often as not with Jeffrey Bernard.

I fell out of love with Bill pretty rapidly and one night I went to the club and 'borrowed' my house keys back. I then went home and phoned him, saying, "Don't come home, all is not forgiven!" His clothes were parcelled up and delivered to his Soho address.

I still saw him for some years afterwards in The Coach and Horses, one of his three favourite Soho hang-outs. He wasn't as handsome any more but I thought of him with great affection. He was a drunk but, after all, he was a lovable drunk.

* * *

During this period I regularly attended Variety Club events, including four consecutive Christmas luncheons at the Savoy Hotel from 1972 to 1975.

The guests ranged from Susan Hampshire, John Mills, Leslie Phillips, Derek Nimmo and Robert Morley to Hylda Baker, Jimmy Jewel, Arthur Askey, Dick Emery and Max Bygraves, not forgetting Eric Sykes, Dora Bryan, Madeline Smith, Ronnie Corbett, Harry Secombe, Michael Crawford, Jimmy Edwards and Frankie Vaughan. One guest I certainly haven't forgotten is Rolf Harris, who also attended every year and sketched one of his lovely caricatures on the back of each menu for me.

I went a bit further afield than the Savoy Hotel when I joined the Swedish actress Camilla Sparv, my great friend Linda Hayden and Catwoman herself, Julie Newmar, on a trip to South Africa. We were there to open various new cinemas in Durban, Cape Town and Johannesburg. This tour isn't one of my favourite memories as we had first-hand experience of the country's political problems.

One day, for example, we were all being driven to Port Torria and sped past a man who'd apparently been run over. We were horrified and, from the back of the limousine, demanded to know why the driver hadn't stopped. He told us that it could well have been an ambush; people were always pretending to be road accident victims in order to stop expensive-looking cars. We could have all been shot, apparently.

CHAPTER ELEVEN

Seventies Sauce

In the spring of 1975 I returned to the Carry On team. And I must say I regretted doing so almost immediately.

I'd left the series 12 years earlier on the advice of my then agent, Dennis Selinger. Barbara Windsor had come in instead and Joan Sims was always there too. However, when the role of a nagging housewife in *Carry On Behind* came up, I felt I wanted to work so I said yes to the old team of Peter Rogers and Gerald Thomas. What really clinched it was the thought of working with Joan, Kenneth Connor and Kenneth Williams again.

Unfortunately, Sid was off doing a play in Australia and I didn't have any scenes with the others. I was with actors who, to me, were complete Carry On strangers. There was Windsor Davies, who hadn't made any Carry Ons previously, and Jack Douglas, who had been in the previous four. It all seemed a bit strange.

Actually, the weather was so bad on location that we spent a lot of the time sitting in our caravans just talking to each other. The German actress Elke Sommer was a real charmer, and was kind enough to give me some posters that she'd had printed up of her paintings. And because there was so much time to sit around, it was on this film that I got to know Kenneth Williams far better than on my three previous Carry Ons.

As it happened I got extremely good billing for *Carry On Behind* – far more prominent than the role deserved – and at least being a Carry On girl again led to a couple of theatre assignments the following year. The original Carry Ons I'd done had been playing on television for several years by then, and there I'd be, grinning and giggling in black-and-white on an almost monthly basis. They would never go away.

Is there one on today? Probably.

* * *

A lot of the films being made in Britain at that time were sex comedies – emphasis on the sex. It all seemed a far cry from the days when some of my own pictures had been considered rather risqué; in fact, the bra and panties scenes, I believe, had sometimes been censored in Ireland! Now, though, producers wanted you to take everything off, and I'd turned down quite a number of films in recent years on that account.

To me, the Confessions and Adventures films were different. I loved making them and it seemed the perfect thing for me to be doing. I wanted to work, of course, but I'd also seen them for exactly what they were – slightly saucier Carry Ons. Now, though, instead of the young dolly bird I was the sexy maternal figure.

And I knew that I didn't need to strip in order to be sexy.

I remember Stanley Long being a little apprehensive about approaching me for *Adventures of a Taxi Driver* in 1975. He told me he never thought an actress of my calibre would accept the job. But I really liked the part. The script was pretty naughty, but outrageously so, and for my tiny role I was to remain fully clothed throughout. Stanley's direction was very playful, and Barry Evans, who played the lead, was a very funny man.

I was a high-class escort who's entertaining a client in the back of the hero's cab. We're circling round and round Leicester Square when the taxi brakes violently and the client shrieks in agony. Instead of showing anything horrid, Stanley just panned across to a cinema hoarding advertising *Jaws*. I thought that was very funny.

I did *Confessions of a Driving Instructor* straight afterwards and that was a very amusing script. I kept my clothes on – not many clothes, maybe, but enough. I was squeezed into a black corselette trimmed with scarlet ribbons, together with black stockings and a black opera hat. I was nipped in at the waist and my bust was thrust forward. This was very sexy underwear, and proved that one really didn't need to take one's clothes off to look sexy.

I did another in the series, *Confessions from a Holiday Camp*, a year later. Those films were helped a lot, I think, by Robin Askwith, who was naughty but very nice and a likable screen presence. He was a good actor too and such fun to be with on the set. He was going out with my friend Linda Hayden at the time and we'd have some great laughs together. There was never a sense of unease or embarrassment with Robin; he just got down to the job in hand and did it brilliantly. The films were saucy but never offensive.

Twelve months after making *Adventures of a Taxi Driver* Stanley Long came back to me for *Adventures of a Private Eye*. The thing I really admired about Stanley and his brother Peter was their interesting approach to casting. In *Private Eye* I was cast alongside Harry H Corbett, Anna Quayle, Jon Pertwee, Willie Rushton and Irene Handl, with Richard Caldicot as the family retainer. So these films certainly attracted some top acting talent, and actors of that quality gave the films a bit of class.

Private Eye was, to my mind, the best in the series. I was playing a batty old lady who rambles on and on about the evils of eating meat. The scenes were well written and I really enjoyed playing them – and again there was no need for any nudity. On my part at least. My good friend Linda Regan had to strip off but then she was a lot younger than me!

Barry Evans was replaced in *Private Eye* by Christopher Neil. But I was back with Barry in what was probably the naughtiest of these films for me, *Under the Doctor*. Around a third of the film was devoted to me as a married woman who seeks a psychiatrist's help with her sexual fantasies. She mistakenly believes that her husband isn't interested in sex and spends her entire time running around in cheeky underwear trying to conjure up some interest in the doctor.

There was a scene in the film in which I had to run round a bed, chasing Barry with a whip. When the director, Gerry Poulson, shouted "Cut," I noticed that I'd 'popped out'.

"You won't keep that in, will you?" I asked.

"I promise you," Gerry smiled, "I won't use that shot."

Liar! That is the only nipple of mine to ever appear on screen – though nowadays nobody would bat an eyelid. Actually, I've only seen *Under the Doctor* once and I don't remember being particularly embarrassed by it.

In 1977 I did one more film of this kind. *Rosie Dixon Night Nurse* was made by the Confessions people and for me was much more innocuous. I played the heroine's mum and was obsessed with newspaper competitions. My husband was played by my old friend from *Rattle of a Simple Man*, John Junkin.

Tragically, Barry Evans, who was so good in *Adventures of a Taxi Driver* and *Under the Doctor*, died several years later – possibly murdered. Dreadful.

* * *

In 1976 Peter Rogers and Gerald Thomas made another Carry On, *Carry On England*. I didn't come back for that one; in fact, I wasn't even asked. But earlier in the year Peter *did* ask me to appear in a stage tour he was sending out. It was a wonderfully awful play called *One of the Family*, and oddly enough it was written by David Pursall and Jack Seddon, the screenwriters of *Carry On England*.

I'd frequently been cast opposite Irene Handl – in fact, I must have worked with her more than anyone else. That was fine by me because I loved her. I'd been her daughter in *I'm All Right Jack*, and in this I was to be her daughter-in-law. Stephen Lewis from *On the Buses* was playing my husband, with Georgina Moon and

David McAlister as our daughter and her new boyfriend. The director was Jan Butlin and the play was all about Irene's outside lav and our efforts to convince her to have an inside one installed. The big pay-off at the end was when we finally got our way! Not a great plot then.

The actress cast as the daughter from next door was occupied with the West End production of *Godspell* at the time so didn't arrive until about a week into rehearsals. We couldn't really get going until then so Irene and I were very curious as to what this young girl might be like. Well, her arrival couldn't have been more dramatic.

This young actress crashed into the rehearsal room wearing a hat, a flowing scarf, some strange kind of skirt, long stripey football socks, odd coloured trainers – and a rather peculiar haircut. Irene and I were aghast as this strange apparition walked in. In the loudest voice possible she bellowed, "Hello-o-o! I hope I'm not late!"

This was Su Pollard. I loved her immediately and we all got on very well while touring *One of the Family*.

There was deep sadness too, however, because during that tour I heard that dear Sid James had died.

It was Monday the 26th of April and we were playing the Salford Hippodrome. After the show the management informed us that Sid had died that evening during his performance in *The Mating Season* at the Sunderland Empire. He had had a heart attack, aged 62. We were all very distressed, especially me. I really cried. I was so upset. Sid and I had worked so much together and I really loved him.

I was also becoming concerned about Irene. She was 74, appearing in a strenuous play, doing bits and bobs in films, and granting interviews to every local newspaper and television station on the tour. On top of all that she was about to do a pilot for television and was trying to learn her lines.

"You really ought to look after yourself," I told her the day after Sid died. "You're overdoing it. Look what happened to Sid. You're always rushing around and you're much older than he was. I think you ought to take it easy."

"Oh Liz," she grumbled. "I'm perfectly all right!"

The play began with me meeting Stephen in the middle of the stage as I straightened his tie. Irene then came on clutching a hot water bottle; she was heading for the outside lav and it was cold in there. And as she came on she said the opening line, yelling "Ethel!" at me. (According to the programme my character was actually called Florrie, but – well, that was Irene for you.) Anyway, just before the curtain went up on this particular night – and this is the night after Sid had died on stage, remember – Irene was waiting in the wings and suddenly started gasping and clutching her chest.

"Oh Liz, oh Liz!" she said. "Oh my God!"

And she collapsed onto the floor.

The curtain swished up – for some reason I vividly remember the fact that it was a curtain that went up rather than to the sides – and of course I had to go on. Well, I was on automatic pilot because I knew we were going to come to a very rapid halt when Irene failed to make her entrance. Stephen came in from the other side, we met in the middle, I straightened his tie – and I whispered, "Irene's just collapsed in the wings."

Stephen went "Oo-er!" in that way he has but then suddenly we heard Irene's voice: "Ethel!" On she came, clutching her hot water bottle. There was nothing wrong with her! She got a big round of applause as usual, though this time she took a different route upstage in order to get a good look at my face. She was an outrageous practical joker.

I had known her for years but she could still fool me. There was a scene later in the play where we had to sit together peeling vegetables, and she frequently made a point of going to the local market earlier in the day and selecting a carrot that looked exactly like a penis!

So when I started peeling I'd find this phallic vegetable rearing up at me from the pile. She must have spent hours and hours going round all the vegetable stalls because these carrots would even have a couple of balls attached. If she was playing a practical joke it had to be perfect. She was always trying to make me laugh but my long experience as a stooge stood me in good stead. I never cracked up once.

One of her best gags happened when we were in Bournemouth. She was still talking about doing this TV pilot and, when I went into her dressing room on the Friday night, I saw that it was completely stripped bare. On tour, of course, actors lay out their make-up in their dressing rooms, pin up their 'Good Luck' cards on the mirror and all the rest of it. But Irene's room was completely empty.

"What's happened?" I asked her.

"Oh, I'm doing that television pilot tomorrow," she said.

"Of course you're not!" I replied. "We've got two shows tomorrow!"

"No, no. Hasn't the company manager told you?"

"Told me? Irene, you've got to be joking! Your understudy is 18 years old!"

So I went roaring round the theatre in search of the company manager.

"Why didn't you tell me that Irene isn't coming in tomorrow?" I screamed.

"What?" he said. "What are you talking about?"

So the two of us went running back to Irene's dressing room – and of course everything had been put back. All the cards were on display again, the make-up and costume were all back in place. And Irene just sat there saying, "What? What is it?"

On another occasion we'd reached the big conclusion to the play and Irene was due to finally sign the agreement to install an indoor lav.

"All right, all right," she'd say. "I'll sign it. Where's the pen?"

In the run-up to this line I looked down at the table and noticed that the all-important pen hadn't been set. I had no lines for a moment so I nipped out of the upstage door and into the wings.

"Where's the pen?" I whispered. "We've got no pen."

The stage manager couldn't find one so I grabbed an eyebrow pencil, thinking the audience wouldn't notice the difference. I quickly tucked it into my sleeve and went back on stage. Everybody looked at me, particularly Irene, who must have been aware that there was a problem because I'd unexpectedly left the stage.

"All right, all right," she said. "I'll sign it. Where's the pen?"

"Oh," I said, "here you are, Gran..."

I slipped the pencil discreetly into her hand, but she took one look at it and cried, "I'm not signing with that! It's an eyebrow pencil!"

She was a real case was Irene Handl.

* * *

In June 1976 Peter Rogers signed me up for a summer season at Scarborough's Royal Opera House. I was to star alongside Jack Douglas, Kenneth Connor and Peter Butterworth in a show called *Carry On Laughing*. The trouble was it meant leaving the tour of *One of the Family* (Joyce Blair took my place) – and Irene wasn't best pleased to see me go.

The *Carry On Laughing* show was delightful, however. The Royal Opera House in Scarborough was a beautiful old theatre and we were re-opening it after it had been dark for nearly five years. I'd worked with Ken Connor on my three Carry Ons back in the early 1960s, as well as in the recent radio comedy *Parsley Sidings*. Peter Butterworth, who'd been in *Carry On Behind* with me, was a joy as well – a very charming, mild-mannered and gentle person. We also had a non-Carry On co-star, Anne Aston, who was very sweet and, at that time, well-known as a hostess on the TV game show *The Golden Shot*.

The play was quite amusing. It was set in a health farm and gave the boys plenty of opportunities to lark about and milk the script for laughs.

There was one scene in which Ken and Peter had to drag up as women, then come back in their normal clothes. But every night one of them would have 'accidentally' kept on his woman's hat, and the audience, thinking this was a genuine mistake, would laugh heartily. But in reality Ken and Peter had worked it all out in rehearsal. People would come up to me in Scarborough and say, "Ooh, I was in on the night when your mate forgot to take the woman's hat off. We did laugh!" And of course I'd play along.

Peter and Ken were true comedy craftsmen and helped make it a wonderful season. Jack Douglas, however, was a problem. Not so much for me, as I didn't have many scenes with him, but I know he bothered Ken and Peter a lot.

As the theatre had just been renovated the dressing rooms no longer had numbers. So Jack went up to Scarborough a little in advance of the rest of us and claimed the best dressing room – the former Number One dressing room – for himself. He put a personalised brass name-plate on the door and even nailed a star to it. The rest of the cast were *really* pissed off about that when they arrived at the theatre.

The main thing that annoyed Ken and Peter, however, was Jack's behaviour during the curtain call each evening. Jack insisted on stepping down from the line after we'd taken our bows, then we all had to stand there like lemons while he thanked the audience personally and announced the fact that his book on honey (!) was being sold in the theatre bar. Peter and Ken repeatedly asked him not to do this, but Jack never listened.

Jack had recently been to an art exhibition and asked if he could have some of the artist's paintings on display in his dressing room, with a view to deciding which one he most wanted to buy at the end of the run.

Well, of course, he just wanted a bit of decoration and had no intention of buying any of them. And when the show was over he just left them in the dressing room; he didn't even send them back!

When Jack left Scarborough he also left behind loads of people whom he'd let down. He'd 'borrowed' a top-notch camera while there, even a Lotus, supposedly in order to test-drive it. He was quite incredible.

Despite this, *Carry On Laughing* was great fun and Scarborough was glorious. It was that very, very hot summer of 1976 – the year of the ladybirds. (They were everywhere.) I hired a beach hut for the season and my good friend that summer was Les Dawson.

We'd known each other ever since Bill directed all his TV shows. Les had kept in touch with me since and now he was appearing in Scarborough for the season. He'd regularly come to my beach hut for a chat, though you couldn't really have a conversation with Les. He'd just talk at you for a couple of hours! Les was impossible, really, but we had some lovely times on the beach. One day we saw some seals in the water, paddled in and stood by them. It was a magical experience – Les actually stopped talking.

He was a dear and very funny man but he was also quite stingey. Bill always used to say that, when they were doing their shows together, Les never bought a round of drinks. And to Bill that was the cardinal sin.

One Saturday Les asked me to dinner along with all the chorus girls from his show. The chorus lines were still quite big in those days – there were at least 12 girls and a couple of other people from his show. During dinner I thought, "My God, Les eats a lot!" He had one large fillet steak, then another large fillet steak... The wines were excellent and I remember being quite surprised at Les' largesse.

The bill then came and was presented to Les at the head of the table. He took out his pen – to sign for it, we assumed. But after a bit of jotting he said, "It comes to £8 each."

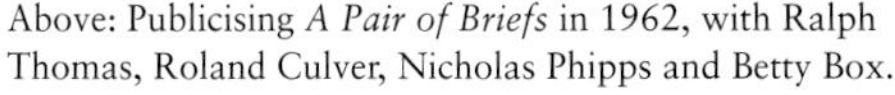

Above: Publicising *A Pair of Briefs* in 1962, with Ralph Thomas, Roland Culver, Nicholas Phipps and Betty Box.

Right: With Joan Greenwood in *The Amorous Prawn*, 1962. What a thrill to act with her!

Below: Working with the lovely Dilys Laye on *Carry On Cruising*, 1962.

Val James and I show off our minks (mine was later stolen). Publicising *Carry On Cruising* in 1962 with Sid, Kenneth Connor and Lance Percival.

With Jennifer Jayne in Acapulco, 1962. One of the most exciting trips of my life.

With James Garner in *The Americanization of Emily*, 1963. My luck was certainly in!

Wedding day with just my Bill – January 1965.

In *Meals on Wheels* at the Royal Court Theatre, 1965. Doesn't everyone wear a balloon?

Me and my MGB opening Britain's first Aero petrol station, 1965. I've always loved cars.

Above: With Patrick Macnee and Diana Rigg in *The Avengers*, 1965. Can I borrow him for a week?

Right: With Busby on the set of *Up the Junction*, 1967. You don't want me to do this film?

Below: With incoming Variety Club Chief Barker Richard Tarling. We've arrived!

Above: With Telly Savalas in *Man and Boy*, 1971. I'm sorry they took your lollipop.

Above right: At the races with Stanley Baker and Benny Hill. Our horse won.

Below: Making *The World About Us* with Captain Sir Ranulph Twisleton-Wykeham-Fiennes, 1971.

Right: Christmas lunches with the Variety Club in the early 1970s. Rolf – I knew you'd be famous one day (which is why I kept them).

The Variety Club
Of Great Britain
(Tent 36)

XMAS
LUNCHEO

Guests of Honour include:

VICTOR BORGE
RONNIE CORBETT
LIZ FRASER
HUGHIE GREEN
SUSAN HAMPSHIRE
ROLF HARRIS
GEOFFREY KEEN
CLIFF MICHELMORE
JOHN MILLS
DEREK NIMMO
MADELEINE SMITH
FRANKIE VAUGHAN

Chairman:
ARKER SIR BILLY BUTLIN, M.B.E.

Introductions by:
BARKER DAVY KAYE

Savoy Hotel, W.C.2
uesday, 9th December, 1975

Above: On stage with Kenneth Connor in *Carry On Laughing*, 1976. Strictly Come Dancing.

Above right: Touring in *Donkey's Years*, 1978. On your bike!

Below: With Harry H Corbett in *Adventures of a Private Eye*, 1976. Look out – someone's coming.

Right: As the Fairy Godmother in *Cinderella* at the Richmond Theatre, 1976. I also had mice in my hair!

Above: With Princess Margaret, Danny La Rue and Frank Carson at a Variety Club event, late 1970s. "It's the way I tell 'em!"

Above (inset): Wearing my Zandra Rhodes dress with the Duke of Edinburgh at another Variety Club event.

Right: As Mrs Lovett on tour in *Sweeney Todd*, 1982. Would you like a piece of pie?

Below: As the dying Mrs Dewey in the TV drama *Eskimos Do It*, 1988. And I live to tell the tale.

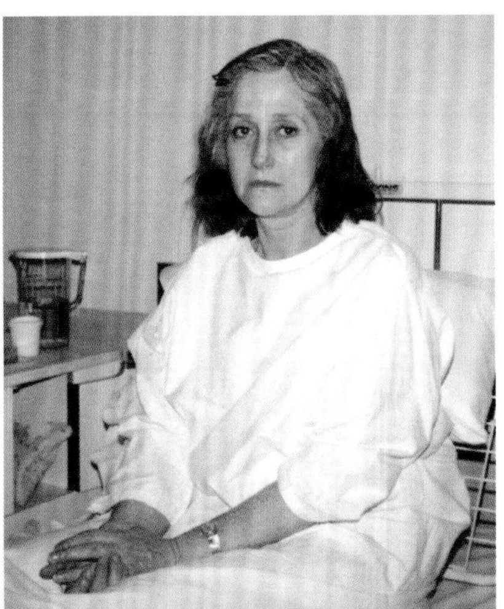

Above: On stage with Gary Webster in *Alfie*, 1992. Just having fun.

Right: Having interviewed Norma Major at Number 10 Downing Street, 1991. I promise I won't talk about John and Edwina.

Below: A hug with two best friends – Roy Hudd and June Whitfield.

As the chorus girls were only earning about £16 a week there was a stunned silence. Then we all started opening our bags and fishing for our money. We all paid equal shares, yet Les had eaten about three times as much as anyone else – and his meals were probably five times as expensive.

I reminded him afterwards that he'd *invited* us to dinner.

"Yes", said Les, "but I didn't say I'd pay!"

So he was a lovely man, but only if you had your own money.

* * *

This bit coming up is for all bridge players. In fact, let's call this little section...

A Bridge Too Far

As a widow I found that very few men really appealed to me. I used to joke that I asked every man I met if he was married, and they always were.

As it turned out, I *did* have an affair with a married man – though, in my defence, his wife was having an affair too, so it seemed OK somehow.

It began shortly before the tour of *One of the Family* started up. Tony Priday was captain of the England bridge team and bridge correspondent for the *Sunday Telegraph*, a wonderful and well-known man who was at the top of his profession. I loved him to bits.

The really romantic thing about Tony was that during my tour he kept in touch with me via his bridge column in the *Sunday Telegraph*. To pass on these coded messages he made me the Queen of Hearts. Wherever we happened to be in any given week, Su Pollard and I would rush into the local newsagent, scrambling to find the *Telegraph* and Tony's latest message. "Read it, Liz, read it!" she'd shout. Quite an excitement for Su and myself on Sundays.

The messages were quite absurd in bridge terms but, when illustrating a hand, he'd write things like

> Although the Queen of Hearts was bare, there were three tricks to lose in five hearts. (25 April)

Another typical message read

> East won with the Queen of Hearts but was obliged to lead a third round of hearts. (2 May)

Among the other ones were

> The lead of the Queen of Hearts would have automatically defeated the contract. (9 May)

> West switched to the Queen of Hearts and suddenly the hand became difficult. (23 May)

> Declarer therefore won the heart lead in hand with the Queen of Hearts and roughed his last diamond with dummy's King of Hearts. (30 May)

It was hilarious to keep finding the Queen of Hearts mentioned in Tony's bridge column on such a regular basis. It was our little secret and it makes me smile even now, thinking that all over the country top bridge aficionados would be reading Tony's bridge column without realising that there, in the middle, was a love letter to Liz Fraser who was on tour in a literally lavatorial play.

Bridge was and is very important to me – I'm a very enthusiastic player. Having an affair with Tony also meant that I had the opportunity to play bridge with him. Also, for P & O I'd go on first-class cruises to Rio and El Salvador, all expenses paid, playing Jeremy Flint, Freddie North and other international bridge celebrities.

The affair with Tony inevitably fizzled out; his wife died and he re-married. We do keep in touch though. We're both Leos; strangely, a lot of my friends have been Leos. He now lives the life of Riley, sailing around the world on cruise ships and talking about his bridge experiences. Though I'll bet he never mentions the Queen of Hearts!

* * *

To round off 1976, I went back into pantomime for the first time in over 20 years. And I absolutely loved it. I was the Fairy Godmother in *Cinderella* at the Richmond Theatre, playing opposite Aimi MacDonald, Roy Kinnear, Julian Orchard, Melvyn Hayes, Bill Pertwee and Sheila White as Cinderella. The really inspired bit of casting, though, was Linda Thorson, who was my on-stage nemesis as an *evil* Dandini and was absolutely outstanding.

It was a traditional pantomime with a perfect cast and a brilliant script. It was also a very lavish production. I had a particularly wondrous costume, all green strips; it was designed by Terry Parsons and really brought out the pagan aspect of the role. I'd add to the costume from time to time and also decorated my hair with various bits and pieces – even my lucky mouse went in there! My most vivid memory, oddly enough, relates to one of my reviews, which called me "the ubiquitous Liz Fraser." I thought this was some extra special bit of praise, and only learned years later that what 'ubiquitous' really meant was that I cropped up in every bloody thing that was going round!

Actually, I have another, much more disturbing memory of that production. Linda had no end of male admirers and one of these guys came to see the show one day accompanied by an equally dashing friend. We went to dinner after the show as a foursome, and at the end of the evening I invited the dashing friend home. OK, so I'm stupid. I'd always thought I'd be able to stay in control in any untoward circumstances, but I was wrong.

Well, this bastard raped me. He'd just assumed I'd be up for it. Well, that was my tag, wasn't it – sex symbol? He left and I felt so ashamed. I'd submitted to something hateful which I couldn't control. I didn't tell a soul; in fact, I didn't even think of it as rape at the time, just 'unwanted intrusion'.

As with all the other horrid things in my life, I just tried to block the memory out.

CHAPTER TWELVE

Gone Bust

In 1977, I had a very good role in an LWT programme called *She*. It was an anthology series of original television dramas focused on strong female characters. My episode was called 'Sight Unseen' and I played an ageing model and actress called Delilah Brown.

She's assigned to a commercial filmed on the barge of a blind young artist called Sam (played by the brilliant Richard O'Callaghan). The camera crew are only there to film her bust because as far as they're concerned the looks have gone; only the figure remains. She's down on her luck so she asks Sam if she can stay with him on the barge. A non-physical relationship develops between them, and the boy is convinced this woman is beautiful. She then becomes worried when he goes off to have an eye operation, and is actually pleased when it's only partially successful. She tries to convince him that she isn't really beautiful, but to him she is and always will be.

It was an hour-long drama directed by Simon Langton and beautifully written by Elizabeth Jane Howard. The ending used to make me well up and I'm getting tearful even now as I remember it. It was an amazing part and allowed me to show that I could really act when given the opportunity. I also appreciated the fact that it was *me* playing this former pin-up girl, which I thought gave the character an added resonance.

Indeed, I was interviewed in *TV Times* and said, "I found the part very difficult to act because I am full of energy, drive and spirit and the woman I play has none of these qualities. I really had to stop myself from thinking there were parallels; I had to pull myself together and say, 'Don't be ridiculous, you're not a has-been, you've got ten more jobs after this one.'"

One of those jobs was a stint at the Duke of York's Theatre in *A Bedfull of Foreigners*, a classic farce by Dave Freeman in which I took over the female lead from June Whitfield as the West End run drew to a close. Lynda Baron, who'd almost got my job on Bournemouth Pier a few years earlier, was also in it, as was David – now Sir David – Jason.

The following year, I did a quick (very quick) cameo in the Sex Pistols film *The Great Rock 'n' Roll Swindle*. The Pistols were apparently big fans of the Carry Ons and were keen to have a sprinkling of Carry On veterans in some scenes set in a cinema. To that end I was signed up alongside Julian Holloway and Irene Handl.

"All you have to do," said the director, Julien Temple, "is walk into the cinema and sit down. Someone in the seat behind annoys you, so you get up and you change seats."

It seemed simple enough and they were paying in cash (which was a first for me). The Pistol involved was guitarist Steve Jones, who was sitting with Mary Millington in the seats behind Julian and me. Our shots were done first and we didn't know exactly what it was Steve and Mary were meant to be doing that was annoying us so much. So we were reacting to nothing really. Then Irene Handl, playing an elderly usherette, shone her torch across and said, "'Ere, what are you two doing?" It was only later that we discovered what Steve and Mary really *were* doing.

During the lunch break I joined Mary for coffee and a sandwich. I thought she was a really nice girl and I was *so* impressed that she owned her own cinema in Soho. "What a great idea," I thought. "Isn't she clever?" I didn't realise, of course, that Mary was a top porn queen and that her cinema screened nothing but blue movies, many of which she starred in. Anyway, Julian and I had left by the time Mary and Steve filmed the scene we were allegedly sitting in front of. It turned out she was 'going down' on him and all sorts!

The Pistols film still hadn't come out when, in August 1979, I read that Mary had committed suicide. She'd become depressed and developed a drug problem, then turned to shoplifting and prostitution to pay for her habit. She was only 33. It was really awful.

* * *

I was then lucky enough to be cast in a touring production of Michael Frayn's *Donkey's Years*, directed by James Roose-Evans. It was a refreshing change to play a spinsterish, bespectacled, middle-aged character. Though I saw a revival of the play at the Richmond Theatre recently and simply couldn't believe that I'd learned that part. It was *so* long.

The cast were refreshing too, particularly George Layton and Nicholas Courtney. George was well known for appearing in sitcoms like *Doctor in the House* and *It Ain't Half Hot Mum*. On tour he seemed to spend all his time scribbling in note pads. I'd ask him what he was doing and he'd say, "Oh, just writing." I took this with a pinch of salt but, of course, he soon became very successful as a TV writer. He created two popular sitcoms of his own, *Don't Wait Up* and *Executive Stress*, as well as writing wonderfully evocative stories of childhood.

Nicholas was something of a cult figure even then. He enjoyed life on the road but to millions he was a television hero as Brigadier Lethbridge-Stewart in *Doctor Who*. Loads of fans would turn up at the stage door and I greatly admired his easy way with them; he treated them with great respect and kindness. Sadly, it was only when he died in 2011 that I learned from his obituaries just how extensive his career had been.

We had a lot of fun together on stage, particularly in Swansea, when the set seemed to take on a life of its own. We shared a very funny scene together, with lots of rapid-fire dialogue, and performed it on a tiny platform on casters. On one particular night we became aware that we were steadily moving forward. We had to keep the dialogue going but, when we realised we were hurtling straight towards the orchestra pit, we thought it might be a good idea to jump off. Which we did – Nicholas flinging himself stage right, me stage left.

The crew had been playing poker in the wings and now they all ran on to drag this platform back into position. So we just started the scene again from the top and received a big round of applause for our pains.

* * *

Reflecting on *Donkey's Years* brings back some unpleasant memories, too. For it was during that tour that I discovered I had breast cancer.

The tour had reached Birmingham and I'd decided to take a bath before turning up at the theatre. As I towelled myself dry I suddenly froze. I'd felt something I really didn't want to feel. There was a small hard lump the size of a pea in my left breast.

There was so much publicity about cancer in those days and I'd been anxious about it for a while. But I'd never bothered to check myself.

I sat down in mild shock, desperately trying to reassure myself that there was nothing wrong. I felt my left breast again and, sure enough, there was a small lump. I told myself not to panic. "Go to the doctor first thing in the morning," I thought. "It'll be fine." With that I turned my attention to the matter in hand, namely the performance that evening.

The following morning I did indeed visit a local doctor, who assured me they'd do a needle test.

"It's probably nothing to worry about," he said, "but do go and see your GP when you get back to London."

Unfortunately, there was nearly a fortnight to wait, as after Birmingham the tour was going direct to Cardiff. That week in Wales was probably the hardest I've ever been through. Every part of me was saying, "For God's sake, just go back to London and see your GP." But my commitment to the show won out and I stayed till the end. And I never mentioned my worries to anyone, because – who knows? – it could have just been a pea!

When I finally saw my doctor I was immediately packed off to the Royal Marsden Hospital in South Kensington to undergo a series of tests. The magical thing about the Royal Marsden is that it's like no other hospital. It has a strange serenity about it. The nursing staff smile all the time and treat all the patients with such understanding and kindness. One nurse stopped me and said, "Miss Fraser! How lovely to see you here!" In a cancer ward! And there was me rigid with fear. But I smiled at the time and I laugh about it now.

Fish swam in tanks. Lamps spraying out fronds of light diverted your attention. And the bar sold Cona coffee and truly delicious sandwiches. As the surgeon poked and prodded at me I felt as if I were on a film set or a stage. This was all too happy and safe and smiley. I was only acting the part of a cancer patient. Other people got cancer, not me. It must be some sort of mistake. But it wasn't.

I was lucky to be seen by the Royal Marsden's head surgeon, Harvey White. I had the mammogram – a very big and rather antiquated machine with your breast squeezed into it until you thought the breast would burst. The results of both that and the needle test were positive.

I was given the options. I could have a complete mastectomy, which the surgeons always preferred because it reduced the risk of the cancer spreading. Or I could gamble and have just the infected tumour removed. This naturally involved the danger that some cancerous cells might be left behind.

I was taken to a room where a nurse showed me all sorts of swimsuits and padded bras designed for one-breasted people. I thought having nothing on one side and a big breast on the other would be intolerable. The decision was doubly difficult for me because, although I considered myself an actress first and foremost, I was well aware that much of my public image was dependent on my large breasts. I couldn't imagine making another Confessions film after such a drastic operation.

I had what were considered enviable breasts. Size 37 double D. And they were natural. These days, of course, you can just buy them; it always seems odd to me that so many girls undergo surgery to have their breasts enlarged. Mine were 100 per cent me. Until now that is, when the surgeons were due to take their share!

In those days pretty much everybody had the whole breast removed, and this was the option that was being recommended to me. I felt completely helpless. I'd have usually discussed such major issues with Bill but he was gone. And I certainly didn't want to burden my elderly mother or my brother with such problems. In fact, I only told a couple of friends.

I decided that, for me, losing my entire left breast would mean losing my identity. My very womanhood was under threat so, in the end, I opted for a partial mastectomy. This would remove the lump and the surrounding tissue. I reasoned that if the surgeon had told me the cancer was widespread then I'd have had no choice other than to have the complete breast removed. However, I *did* have a choice. Nobody knew whether the cancer would reappear or not and I felt that, if I was unlucky, I could always have another operation.

So, being a gambler, I went for the lumpectomy. Don't forget this was 1978 and at that time the risks were much higher. But once I'd come to the conclusion that it could be removed bit by bit if the need arose, I felt a lot better. In fact, my chief concern was for the little Basset Hound puppy I'd recently ordered at the Cardiff dog show.

"Look, I've ordered this puppy," I said to Harvey White. "Should I have it or not?"

"No," he replied rather ominously. "Actually, I don't think that's a good idea."

I was really asking if I was going to live, of course. And there was my answer. He obviously thought there was a strong possibility that I'd die. I never for one moment thought I would and, in fact, his reaction was exactly the slap in the face I needed.

I thought, "Stuff it! I'm going to have that dog."

And I did. This was Banjo Basset (the one with the tidy balls, if you remember) and he was with me throughout my treatment. For me, he became a symbol of my fight against cancer.

Later I realised that no surgeon can look his patient in the eye and tell them they're going to be fine. He has to be honest, within reason, and make it clear that there's always a chance things will go wrong. Still, the thought of Banjo Basset together with my positive outlook on life saw me through.

In fact, by the time I went into hospital I'd become remarkably philosophical about it all; whatever would be would be and there was absolutely nothing I could do about it. I'm a very emotional person and can cry at the drop of a hat. But I've always had a large reserve of physical courage too. I'm also an actress and, I think, a good one. I can put a brave face on things.

I was certainly used to dealing with contracts so when I had to sign the hospital release form I went through every detail with a fine-toothed comb. In the section where you gave the surgeon permission to undertake the operation, I wrote in bold lettering 'NO MASTECTOMY' and initialled it. I then wrote 'NO OTHER SURGEON' because I wanted Harvey White to do it no matter what.

As with acting, once the business side was sorted out I had to give the performance. At that point I brought out the bravest brave face I'd ever put on. In reality my legs were like jelly when I arrived at the hospital. But as the nurses wheeled me to the operating theatre I joked and laughed with them. I'd also prepared a special message for my surgeon. I'd pinned a badge to my gown which read, "If you don't want the goods, don't muck them about!" We both laughed about that.

In the days following the operation I was surrounded by all my dearest friends. They did everything they could to make things as pleasant as possible. I wasn't supposed to drink but Linda Thorson took me across the road for champagne. I came back and was promptly sick. It was my own fault but it was such fun!

Despite all this kindness, it was one of the other patients (there were only two) in that tiny ward who inspired me the most. To be honest, her daily routine had begun to get on my nerves slightly. She'd ask for a bowl so that she could wash, then she would carefully apply full make-up. After that she'd place Carmen rollers in her hair and lovingly manicure her nails. Only then would she face the day, even if that day involved nothing more than sitting in bed and doing the *Times* crossword.

She seemed happy and content, and I said as much to one of the nurses.

The nurse smiled and said, "Sadly, that lady is dying."

I couldn't believe it. Obviously that little ritual was her way of coping. She'd come to terms with her impending death but wasn't going to let it drag her down. She faced death with dignity, and indeed she did die soon afterwards.

We should all appreciate the fact that life is very precious.

* * *

After the tumour had been removed I had to endure ten weeks of very painful radium treatment. I was cauterised repeatedly and had gauze strapped round my left side. I'd wear a trouser suit and a huge cotton blouse so nobody could see how ill I was. And I told no one in the business about my 'big C' because I thought it would stop people employing me.

In fact, I managed to do a few television jobs during the last weeks of the treatment. I went through the motions of playing the charades game *Give Us a Clue* and nobody suspected a thing. I even did an episode of *Robin's Nest* and that was the worst experience of my acting life. I joked along with Richard O'Sullivan, Tessa Wyatt and Tony Britton on set but I felt so dreadfully ill. I'm sure I looked dreadful too, but, again, nobody knew and I fulfilled the contract.

My problems were then compounded by the discovery that the lump that had been removed was only a secondary tumour. Worse still, they couldn't *find* the primary one. It was a very dangerous situation, for if that cancer was eating away inside me and they didn't find it pretty quickly, it might be too late to do anything about it. After all, my surgeon had told me that if I'd ignored the lump in my left breast it would have become terminal after six months.

The only thing for it was to undergo more tests. These were conducted over a ten-day period at several different hospitals. I became something of a medical mystery. Amazingly, they never found that elusive tumour and concluded it had simply disappeared without trace. What a relief!

I had to report back to the Royal Marsden every three months for routine checks. In the meantime I did an episode of *The Professionals*, playing a lady fence. This was a very nice job; Martin Shaw and Lewis Collins were very welcoming to me and great to act with.

But then, about a year after the operation, I went back to the hospital in a terrible panic. I'd found another lump in the same breast. My surgeon decided to remove the affected area as quickly as possible. He made sure to cut along the original incision, thus keeping scarring to a minimum.

All things considered, I felt amazingly well. So much so that I agreed to take part in an *All Star Gala* at the Alexandra Theatre in Birmingham. I was on the same bill as Ken Dodd, Fenella Fielding,

Derek Nimmo and Wayne Sleep, among others, and it was directed by that excellent actor Alan Curtis. I even signed up for a celebrity edition of *It's a Knockout*. Frustratingly, my agent had told the producer I wasn't 100 per cent so I was given all the least physical games to take part in. But at least I *did* take part.

I knew, of course, that the producer was only trying to be kind. In fact, I was asked back the following year and this time, to my great delight, he had me climbing up greasy poles and jumping through tyres while carrying plates of cream. I was as rough and tumble – and messy – as everybody else and it felt fantastic. I was tough and strong and more determined than ever to prove that cancer isn't a death sentence.

* * *

With this in mind I ventured out on tour again in the summer of 1980.

The play was a hilarious cricketing comedy by Richard Harris called *Outside Edge* and the cast – including Jimmy Ellis, Imogen Hassall and Norman Rossington – was a very happy one. Norman was extremely fond of Banjo Basset. In every theatre we went to he'd go up to the microphone and shout "Banj! Banj! Come and find me, Banj!" And the dog would career all around the theatre to try and find him.

By this time I'd put together a new dog act. I'd introduce "Banjo the Magnificent Basset!" and there he'd be, sitting on a trolley, looking mournfully out at the audience. "Ladies and Gentlemen," I continued, "this is a dog act. You might think it's odd having a Basset Hound doing a dog act but I really didn't want an Alsatian or a Pit Bull terrier as I thought they'd be too vicious. So instead of that I would like to introduce you to my docile colleague Banjo."

At this point he'd growl and go for me, pretending to savage my out-stretched hand. He did it every time and it was very funny. We did that act in a number of benefit shows and a few TV programmes too, including *Pebble Mill at One* in Birmingham.

The *Outside Edge* tour was a very long one and I could only manage it in six-week bursts. In fact, I had to drop out halfway – returning later – when I underwent a third operation to remove more cancerous cells from my left breast, reducing it even further. I was staying with some friends in Buckinghamshire at the time, which was handy for paying daily visits to the Royal Marsden. I'd developed an infection so they'd insert a great big syringe and suck out a horrible yellow substance. I had no idea what it was. Best not to know.

But I loved *Outside Edge* and was determined to keep going. I relished the role of Miriam and tried to bring out the hidden sadness of this apparently contented 'cricket widow'. I understood this woman and added bits of 'business' to show that, despite appearances, her life was actually made of straw.

The great sadness of that first leg of the tour was Imogen Hassall. She was quite brilliant in the play and looked radiant throughout. Yet she took a fatal overdose in November of that year. It was a cry for help that, sadly, no one heard.

When I returned to the run, Jimmy Ellis had left and Geoffrey Davies had come in as my husband instead. The last stop on the tour was the Cambridge Arts Theatre and just before the final performance we were told that the producer, Bill Kenwright, had no further use for the set – and it was indeed on its last legs.

Because the play ended with Miriam throwing things at her husband, we were told that, if we fancied, we could literally destroy the set. Just imagine it – being given the chance to smash up a whole set while the audience were still watching! It was like being a rock star.

The scoreboard was the first prop to get the treatment. Then the cabinet where the cricket bats were kept was knocked for six. Right at the very end, as the row reached its crescendo, Geoffrey and I absolutely went for it. We both grabbed cricket bats and smashed up everything in sight. There was no set left when the curtain came down.

When Geoffrey and I came out of the stage door that night we were stopped by an American couple who'd come round to thank us.

"Gee," they said. "We thought that ending was the most fantastic thing we've ever seen on stage. And you do that every night?"

We didn't disillusion them.

* * *

Immediately after finishing in *Outside Edge* I went into another stage production, this time at the Churchill Theatre. I'd previously played Bromley in a revival of *The Little Hut* with Gerald Flood and Edward de Souza. This time it was another revival, of Terence Rattigan's wartime play *Flare Path*. It was directed by Patrick Lau and had an excellent cast comprising Judy Geeson, Desmond Carrington and Brian Miller.

This was a super, heartbreaking part for me. I was playing Doris, a cockney barmaid who's married to a Polish count; he's an airman and in the final scene she hears that he's been killed in action. This drained me emotionally every night. He's left a letter to her in Polish and, because she can't read it, she gets someone to translate it for her. Until that letter is read out, she's never been convinced her husband really loved her. And I'd break down at every performance. There was really no acting required on my part at all. I'd be in floods of tears and when I returned to my dressing room, my face was absolutely black from the mascara that had run. I must have looked a sight at the curtain calls.

I was still having check-ups at the Royal Marsden, though only every six months now, and during the *Flare Path* run my surgeon, Harvey White, came to see the show with his wife. When I'd left hospital the first time round Harvey had given me a note which read, "To the best patient I ever had." And over the years we'd become friends. I'd even spent a holiday with his family at their cottage in Ireland.

Anyway, we went out to an Indian restaurant after the performance and Harvey said, "Well, of course, you'll never get cancer there again because of the clostridium perfringens bacteria." (I phoned him while writing this to check the spelling!) I asked him what he meant and he said, very matter of factly, "You had gangrene."

"I had gangrene?" I said. "But you die from that, don't you?"

"Well," he smiled, "obviously not in your case. But you'll never get cancer there again. Gangrene kills off all the cells."

So, against all the odds, I'd pulled through.

* * *

I may not have stopped working but I *did* occasionally stop myself from buying inappropriate clothing. After all, one breast was now much smaller than the other. Nobody really noticed because I wore good bras and the right clothes. But sometimes I'd be looking at a tight-fitting blouse and I'd say to myself, "No Liz, you can't have that. You'll be able to see the difference."

Nearly a year had gone by since my third operation when Harvey said to me that I was now well enough to have a cosmetic procedure, reducing the size of the right breast to match the one on the left. Luckily, the Royal Marsden was playing host to the top cosmetic surgeon for a month and, 118 stitches later, I emerged with two more or less matching breasts.

I'd always been self-conscious about my big breasts anyway. Now that they'd been reduced out of medical necessity, I felt comfortable and happy. Though to this day the right one still tends to put on more weight than the left!

* * *

I was thinking recently of my various hospital visits over the years and came up with the following.

Hospitals – I've had a few
But not too few to mention

Scarlet fever aged three
I still remember the wrapped red blanket –
Guy's
Tonsils aged six – St Thomas's
Mastoids at seven – Brooke Street

Hysterectomy (too early for me to have children) –
Northwick Park
Marsden three times (thank you!)
Hammersmith Hospital – pace-maker
Ealing – parathyroid gland whipped out
Charing Cross for back, feet and ears

I'm sort of bionic
Outlived friends who lived blameless lives
And now I only visit the vet
(Too many, expensive times)

All the above on the National Health
Fortunate to live in London!

CHAPTER THIRTEEN

Out and About

Sadly, it was during the run of *Flare Path*, in October 1980, that my mother died.

She never knew I had cancer and I was glad. She was a kind and lovely lady who'd worked hard to give me a good education.

God bless her.

* * *

Bill Kenwright was to prove the most important figure in my stage career during the 1980s. The roles were always good and the productions were always done on a shoestring; that was part of Bill's charm. I'd done *Outside Edge* for him in 1980 and now he came through with another offer.

Murder Mistaken was a bit of an old potboiler but it was an enjoyable tour to do. The director was Harvey Ashby and there was a lovely cast on board, including Joyce Blair, Chili Bouchier and my old chum from Bournemouth Pier, MacDonald Hobley. Bill, of course, was being his usual 'careful' self. I really like him, but just occasionally his cost-cutting habits would threaten the credibility of a play. This one, for example.

The starting point of the play was that a young husband had murdered his wife by putting her head into a gas fire. I thought nothing of this until we all went for our costume fittings and were given contemporary clothes.

I said to Bill, "We can't do this play in modern dress, you know."

"Why not, Liz?" he sighed.

"Because they stopped all that in 1974. It isn't possible to gas yourself nowadays."

I knew this because of my experience with the Samaritans. In fact, I explained in great detail that once North Sea gas came in the gas used for heating was no longer poisonous. So it was now impossible to kill yourself or be killed by a domestic appliance.

"Oh God, Liz!" Bill moaned. "Only you would think of that. This is going to cost me a fortune!"

So off we all went to the costume hire departments rather than looking through the Littlewoods catalogue. It made the play much more authentic and I very much enjoyed the role of the rich, brash and loud-mouthed widow. I got good reviews wherever we went, and I was particularly flattered when the author of the play, Janet Green, sent me a note saying that I was the best Freda Jeffries she'd seen. And that included Margaret Lockwood, who played her in the film version.

It was during this tour – at the Alexandra Theatre in Birmingham, in fact – that I was told by the company manager one day that the Kenwright office had asked me to ring them. This was just before the Wednesday matinée and I wanted to finish my make-up first. I then rang the office and was told that my brother Philip had been found dead that morning.

He was then the manager of the Epsom branch of Waitrose and hadn't arrived that morning with the keys. The police had to force his front door and found him lying dead on the bed. He'd had a heart attack.

The news hit me hard but the curtain was due to go up in a matter of minutes. The audience were already seated. So I went on and cried more or less throughout the performance, adding to the dialogue with "Oh, I've got this dreadful cold!" and such like. Anything to cover up the crying. And do you know what was so ridiculous? I still got laughs in all the right places.

How I got through this period I really don't know. My mother had died only six months before and now all I had left were two cousins. I had to carry on in the show for the remainder of the week and finally arrived at Philip's council house on the Sunday. It broke my heart. A trifle was still sitting on the kitchen table, together with a cold pot of tea. The fridge was stocked with all his favourite cakes and the bath still had water in it, with the bath mats laid out on the floor. And on the bed in the spare room was an open suitcase with new pyjamas and pants in it. He'd been due to go away with friends on the Saturday.

I also realised, from looking at various magazines he had, that Philip had been a homosexual. I remembered that long ago he'd had a very close friend called Derek who'd died very young, and how upset Philip had been about it. As far as I was aware, he'd never had a partner since. Sorting through his clothes and effects made me love him all the more, and I gained a clearer understanding of the differences we'd had over the years. All I took away was a small table and a set of pink tea things.

* * *

Later that year Bill Kenwright came up trumps again, offering me a touring production of a very funny Mike Harding play called *Fur Coat and No Knickers*. Trouble was, it was all about a north country family and I'd never done a northern accent. To make matters worse we actually opened in Manchester!

Fortunately, the other cast members – all of them genuine northerners – were very helpful, particularly Ivan Beavis, who as well as being my leading man was also something of a local hero. In the end, even Mike Harding himself seemed convinced. I starred in several different runs of the play, playing at one point opposite two very talented youngsters, Peter Howitt and Louise English.

There were a couple of incidents during that tour that stick in my mind. The first was at the Alexandra Theatre in Birmingham again. (Why is it always Birmingham?) I'd driven up the M1 in foggy conditions, only to be told on my arrival that two of the actors hadn't turned up; they were stuck in the fog. And one of these absentees was the first person to come on after a long monologue of mine that began the play. Because these two characters didn't have their own understudies, the company manager decided there was nothing for it but to have two people go on and *read* the parts. He would be one of the readers and my understudy would be the other.

Well, the announcement was made and from the wings I could hear all the muttering and groaning from the disappointed audience. And I couldn't blame them. The opening monologue involved me massaging my feet, so this time I went on stage, took off my shoes and said, "Ooh my feet! I've walked all the way up the M1 to be 'ere on time, I 'ave. *I* got here but the rest of 'em bloody 'aven't!"

The audience loved it and it became a running gag. When the readers came on, for example, I said things like "Have you got the right page, love? Ee, isn't it dreadful about the others? They're still coming up the M1, you know!" And so on.

My old friend Bernard Miles – Lord Miles by then – happened to be in the audience that night. He came round afterwards and said how glad he was the others hadn't turned up because the performance had been hilarious. He was planning a revival of an old Mermaid hit, the Lionel Bart-Laurie Johnson musical *Lock Up Your Daughters*, and offered me the role of Mrs Squeezum on the spot. Because of the tour I had to turn him down, which was a shame because Laurie, of course, was a very dear friend.

The other incident involved none other than Banjo Basset, who at the Cambridge Arts Theatre succeeded in finding his way on stage while we actors were performing on a rostrum. There was no way we could get down to shift him, and all the time he just looked out at the audience with that wonderfully doleful expression of his.

In the end the poor company manager had to come on stage and remove Banjo personally.

* * *

Another of my Bill Kenwright dates was less amusing. We were due to perform *Murder Mistaken* in Belfast. This was 1981, remember – Bobby Sands was in the middle of his hunger strike and bombs were going off all over the city. The situation was so grave that Equity had given us the option of pulling out of this particular date.

A company meeting was called and we decided to do it after all. I think a couple of the actors were unsure, but I for one felt that, though this play was hardly the best in the world, there was no reason why we shouldn't take it to Belfast.

When we got there we were given a police escort to and from the theatre. And the Europa Hotel, which was directly opposite our digs, was bombed. But we got through the opening performance without mishap, and at the end the audience rose to their feet and clapped and clapped. This standing ovation went on for five minutes – it was the audience's way of saying, "Thank you for coming!" – and all of us in the cast cried and cried.

We were very proud that we had gone there. Sadly, after his long fast, Bobby Sands died just a few days after we left.

Six years later I was back in Belfast for a Kenwright tour of *Oliver!* This time, thankfully, the 'troubles' seemed much less dramatic than on the previous occasion. This tour was a lovely, year-long engagement in a musical I knew well and really liked. Because it featured very complex sets we had to take up residence at each theatre for a month or so at a time – which was lovely because that way you could get a feel for each city and really settle in. Though Widow Corney was a relatively small part for me, I was still given second billing to the incomparable Victor Spinetti, who was quite brilliant as Fagin.

I reached Belfast by ferry and was given a bottle of Dom Perignon by the captain to drink on opening night. In Belfast at that time you were allowed to take your own wine into restaurants, so I gave the champagne to the theatre manager, asking him to keep it in the fridge during the performance.

Afterwards, he came running over to me in panic and said, "Oh Liz, I'm terribly sorry. I put that bottle in the freezer and it's just blown up!"

Champagne? In the freezer?

Mind you, I suppose this was no more stupid than me storing Château Lafite in the immersion heater!

* * *

Probably the most fun I had on a Kenwright tour came in the summer of 1982, when Bill sent out a revival of Noël Coward's *Fallen Angels*, directed, once again, by Harvey Ashby. In this one, Dora Bryan and I had some big boots to fill, as the most famous production of the play had starred Hermione Gingold and Hermione Baddeley.

I adored touring with Dora. We'd lodge together and she'd always leave it to me to pick our digs. She had a dog called Lottie and I had Banjo, of course, so we'd tour with the two dogs. Actually, I came in halfway through the tour, substituting for Hildegarde Neil, and Dora was very helpful when I first took over, giving me lots of useful tips.

In one scene we had to play drunk and there was a great deal of comedy business involved. When we came off on the first night Dora said to me, "When you light my cigarette I want you to go further down."

I said "OK," so the next night I held the cigarette lighter lower than I had before. But when we came off she gave me the same note. This went on night after night, with me holding the lighter lower and lower each time. I wondered what on earth she was playing at. Eventually she was having to squat down so low that her face was only six inches off the floor. The audience were in hysterics.

Anyway, when we came off this final time she said, "No no, Liz. I meant lower downstage!"

What she'd actually wanted was for me to light the cigarette downstage so she could be upstage for her next speech. Why it took her so long to explain I don't know. But the audience loved it.

There were some typical Kenwright economies in evidence on *Fallen Angels*. In one scene Dora and I, drunk again, had to eat oysters. To start with we had a real half-lemon wrapped in gauze. However, a couple of weeks into the run the lemon was replaced by a piece of sponge wrapped in muslin. This, as you can imagine, tasted foul. Dora and I went to the company manager and were told a fresh lemon per performance was too expensive!

And indeed we never did have one again until the final week, which was in Taunton. It was the very last performance and we suddenly realised we were squeezing a real lemon onto these oysters.

It was quite bitter so I pursed my lips and said, "Ooh, we've got a real lemon tonight!"

And Dora did the same. "Oh my goodness, so we have!" she cried. "How long is it since we had a real lemon?"

"A *real* lemon?" I replied. We were both sucking in our cheeks and pursing our lips by now. "Oo, I can hardly talk!"

"Neither can I!"

We ad-libbed like this for something like five minutes and the audience were in stitches.

I told Bill about it many years later. "You couldn't even afford a real lemon," I said. He denied it, of course.

The big joke whenever you were on a Kenwright tour was that as soon as you arrived at the Liverpool Empire the rumours would go round that Bill himself would be in the audience that week; it was his home town, after all. You soon realised, however, that when Bill was in Liverpool it certainly wasn't to see his own production. He was there to watch Everton play football. As a result I started supporting Liverpool and have done ever since.

I thought, "Sod it! If he's going to support Everton then I'm going to support Liverpool!"

Actually, football is quite a big part of my life. I also support Sunderland, Newcastle and Bolton and have all the sports channels on TV, watching or recording most games. In fact, I was in a taxi not long ago and the driver remarked that I was the first female he'd ever had in his cab that he could talk football to.

* * *

As well as joining football clubs, I found that touring was also good for buying houses!

I'd have a lot of free time during the day and, while playing in Bournemouth, I wandered into an auction and in no time at all became the owner of a chalet house on top of Canford Cliffs. It looked lovely for future holidays and today would be worth millions. However, I sold it at a profit soon afterwards because, not only were my weekends there few and far between, but also Banjo Basset would just disappear the minute I opened the door to let him out. I'd then have to spend hours searching for him.

Then in Brighton one week I came across a huge mock-up of a beautiful new complex that was being built on the Marina. I became convinced that this would be just the right place for a widow to meet all those wonderful men anchoring their boats and having glasses of champagne and enjoying the good life. And Dora lived nearby with her cricketer husband, Bill, so it seemed perfect.

But by the time the complex was finished, the bubble had burst. Brighton and particularly the Marina were empty; the whole thing was dead in the water, so to speak. My £70,000 flat dropped in value to only £40,000. I stayed there a couple of times and then rented it out. I hung onto it for a decade or so, by which time Brighton had picked itself up and I was able to sell it for about the same price as I had purchased it.

Dora and Bill owned Clarges, a lovely old hotel on the seafront which they'd started converting into flats. An excellent idea at the time but, again, a very expensive one as Brighton went into recession. It became a huge debt for them, so to keep afloat Dora never stopped working – frequently with me.

I settled ultimately in Fulham and, thanks to the Stock Market, had three different properties that I let out. This gave me the chance to take on the stage work that really challenged me and that I loved to do. I honestly think the theatre has given me the very best acting opportunities of my life.

* * *

After *Fallen Angels*, I went on an Arts Council tour of *Sweeney Todd*, co-starring with Brian Murphy, who had played the title role before at the Theatre Royal Stratford East. I was cast as Mrs Lovett the pie-maker and absolutely adored it. I think she may well be my favourite part. It was something to really sink one's teeth into, if you'll pardon the pun.

Stephen Sondheim had added music to the legend but ours was the original, unadorned, blood-spattered melodrama – no songs for us. We had a lone pianist tucked away in the pit and the proscenium was draped with a heavy blood-red curtain. The reviews were brilliant, and they weren't confined to local papers either, which is unusual for a tour. The *Daily Telegraph* called me "an appalling delight," which may sound like a funny sort of compliment but I was quite happy with it.

One play I gratefully missed out on was *Steaming*, which was written by Nell Dunn of *Up the Junction* fame. At first, I was thrilled to be offered an opportunity to go with this show to New Zealand. Not only did I have a good friend there who'd lived near me before she emigrated, but I also wanted to see the country.

Well, I read the Samuel French edition of the play and thought it excellent. But when I got to New Zealand I found that the script had been adapted for local audiences and the dialogue was now full of extremely nasty expletives. The whole production was very crude. After rehearsing for about ten days I knew that I couldn't continue. I also knew the producer would have no trouble replacing me as the actress who'd played the part in Australia was available.

Obviously it wasn't good for one's reputation to drop out of a production, and I was sorry not to have seen more of New Zealand. But it was a decision I never regretted. Especially when my friend sent over the reviews, all of which, without exception, pointed out that Liz Fraser had made a very wise decision when she went back to London.

Another wise decision was to go back into pantomime, which I really adored. I popped up – usually in a cloud of dry ice – in Doncaster, Oxford and twice in Leatherhead. I was as often as not cast as the Fairy Godmother in *Cinderella*, though I also played the Empress of China in *Aladdin* with Rodney Bewes, Christopher Beeny and Sophie Lawrence. That was fun but the Fairy Godmother was my favourite.

At the Apollo Theatre in Oxford the character was renamed Fairy Story-Teller Flibberty Gibbet and I wrote all my own dialogue. One review pointed out that the script was very poor *except* for the Fairy's lines, which can't have pleased the original writer. Jim Davidson was a brilliant Buttons, and he was great with the kids, but towards the end of the run he told us that he'd arranged a midnight matinée in which we could all be as rude as we liked.

He subsequently made a good business out of staging full-scale smutty pantomimes and this was his first attempt. Rather than being rude, I decided to play the Fairy as if she was absolutely pissed. I lurched around the stage, with bottles hidden all over the set, and got even more laughs than usual. At the very end I yelled out, "And I wrote all my own lines. Every single line I've said was written by me..."

The only person who wasn't laughing was the writer, who, unknown to me, was in the audience that night.

CHAPTER FOURTEEN

Back on the Tube

As well as enjoying panto, I also appeared in a couple of big musicals. I've mentioned *Oliver!* already, but a few years before that I appeared in *Annie*, which I thoroughly enjoyed. In fact, the alcoholic orphanage matron Miss Hannigan remains one of my favourite roles.

The show was put on at the Belgrade Theatre in Coventry and in the small role of a police officer was a local man called Dave Willetts. He had quite a well-paid 'proper' job, together with a wife and children, but was keen to make it in the theatre. I told him this wasn't a great idea as it's so difficult to get established in showbusiness. A few years later, I was absolutely thrilled, and even a bit tearful, when I went to see him playing the title role in the West End production of *The Phantom of the Opera*.

It wasn't all theatre in the mid-1980s. I was getting some interesting work on TV too. Not as much as I would have liked, perhaps, but interesting all the same.

There was the P D James mystery *Shroud for a Nightingale* for Anglia Television, which was an excellent series. Roy Marsden, as Commander Dalgliesh, was charming and I loved being in Norwich. I also loved not knowing who did it; we didn't see the final script until well into production, so I was hoping it would be me!

I also did two series of the Channel 4 comedy *Fairly Secret Army* and travelled up to Birmingham for Central's *Hardwicke House*.

I did that one mainly because my old friend Roy Kinnear was starring as the headmaster. I was cast as his slovenly secretary. I'd recently broken my leg and had to do the whole thing with plaster up to my knee. I therefore made the hectic journey to the studio by train and was hopping around on crutches throughout the filming.

The show was set in a comprehensive school and proved so controversial it was cancelled after only two episodes had gone out; the other five have never been transmitted. I didn't think it was that shocking myself but it was quite exciting to have been in something that was deemed so offensive.

Sadly it turned out to be one of Roy's last appearances as about 18 months later he had a fatal accident in Spain during the making of *The Return of the Musketeers*. He would have been very proud today to see how well his actor son Rory is doing.

One of my very favourite television roles came along in 1986. It was an episode of *Miss Marple* called 'Nemesis'. Joan Hickson was quite splendid as Miss Marple and the show was a joy to do. It was a very sad little scene but I realised straight away that this character, Mrs Brent, was someone I could really bring to life. She wasn't just sad in this scene but also very drunk. Glamour fading and close to tears over her dead daughter. It was what they call a showy role – not long on screen but capable of making a big impact if you play it right. So I really wanted to do the part justice.

It was only a one-day assignment in Oxford, and when I got there one of the actors took me aside and said, "The director makes you do it over and over again. It's enough to drive you insane!"

But I was unfazed by this. After all, I liked the character, I knew the part, it was such a great scene and it was a gift, really. So we went onto the set, the camera came in very close on me and I did the scene right the way through. Tears rolled down my cheeks and I finally asked my companion, John Horsley as the professor, if he would like another drink. That was the end of the scene and the end of the take.

Sure enough the director said, "We'll go for another take. Let's do it from a different angle."

But the cameraman said to him, "No. You've got it all there in one. I don't think that can be improved upon. May I just suggest we do a two-shot as a cut-away?"

And that's what they did. So that *Miss Marple* performance was all done in one take. Just the first take and done. I couldn't help crying; it was so sad.

When it was repeated recently a neighbour of mine saw it and said, "I didn't know you could act!"

Curse of the Carry Ons.

* * *

I'd started talking about my cancer experience by this time, simply because I wanted other women to be aware of the dangers. So as an actress I simply had to take on the challenge of a wonderful script that the BBC asked me to do in 1988.

The play was called *Eskimos Do It* and, to this day, no other piece has got across the horror of cancer so perfectly. It was a first TV play by Jim Barton and the title was explained in my character's line, "Eskimos do it, you know. They walk out into the snow when their time has come."

Comedy talents are underrated – you have to cry or die before you're taken seriously in this business. So when I was given the part of Mrs Dewey in *Eskimos Do It* it seemed like a lifeline and a dream come true. She was suffering through the latter stages of stomach cancer and had only two weeks to live – and knew it.

The fact that I had once had cancer myself was irrelevant. I was playing a character who knew she was going to die, whereas I never thought, even for a moment, that I would.

Usually, a serious drama of this sort would be offered to Judi Dench or Maggie Smith, but the director, Derek Lister, went for me and Jean Boht instead. The *Daily Telegraph* critic Richard Last pointed out that

> As a piece of television, *Eskimos Do It* – a reference to the spontaneous euthanasia allegedly practised in the far North – compelled unblinking attention. Its strengths lay in its simplicity and recognisable ordinariness. Mrs Bing and Mrs Dewey, two beautifully unaffected performances from actresses normally associated with comedy, were comfortable suburban widows, not victims of grand tragedy. Proverbial hearts of stone must have been moved.

Though it was a truly harrowing piece, I was so thrilled at being given such an excellent opportunity that I actually laughed on the way home from filming. I was so excited I alerted lots and lots of producers when the play was about to be transmitted. I was hopeful that similar serious roles might follow. Unfortunately, it didn't work out that way, so I had to content myself with a clutch of good reviews. One of them remarked that "Jean Boht and Liz Fraser give two of the TV performances of the year." Many critics expressed surprise at the fact that I could do something so serious, but they were still gratifying.

It was without doubt the best thing I'd done on television for years and remains the performance I'm proudest of. The BBC were obviously pretty proud of the programme as a whole because Jean and I were invited onto the *Wogan* chat show on the evening the play was transmitted, which gave me a chance to talk about my own battle with cancer.

* * *

The following year I went to Pinewood for a couple of films. In *The Lady and the Highwayman* I played an old hag called Flossie – with plenty of warts and looking (hopefully) unrecognisable. Then in

Chicago Joe and the Showgirl I played opposite Kiefer Sutherland and Emily Lloyd; the latter, I remember, spent a lot of time making sure her eyelashes and fingernails were just right.

Also around this time I was making TV shows like *Rude Health*, *The Bill* and *Birds of a Feather*, because to some extent I'd fallen out of love with stage work. It had given me some great experiences but I'd recently been shaken by the deaths of several old friends. To make matters worse, all of them seemed to have died while performing on stage. There was Sid, of course, followed by Peter Butterworth, Tommy Cooper, Eric Morecambe… All of them going the way they did was truly shocking, and I decided I didn't want to go the same way. I didn't want to sit down on stage one night and never get up again for the next line!

Even so, in 1992 I couldn't resist an offer from director Lawrence Till to play Ruby in his revival of *Alfie* at the Octagon Theatre in Bolton. It was quite a small role, but Shelley Winters had made such an impact in the film version that I wanted to tackle it. I also doubled as the doctor so I was on stage quite a lot and relished the challenge.

One local reviewer was kind enough to say I gave "a hysterically funny performance" as Ruby. But the best thing about this production was Gary Webster as Alfie. He was already a hit on TV (in fact, around the same time I appeared with him in an episode of *Minder*), and he strutted around the stage with all the arrogance the role demanded. This, together with a lovely pop soundtrack and Ethne Brown's haunting performance as Lily, made the show a brilliant evocation of 1960s London.

Lawrence turned out to be one of the best directors I've worked for. He subsequently produced one of Channel 4's biggest successes of recent years, *Shameless*. For a time I kept asking him why he'd never used me on that show. Then I watched it and realised that the cast was a fixed set of family characters – and all of them were doing the kind of things I didn't think you could get away with on British television. So I didn't ask again!

Shortly after doing *Alfie* I signed on for the TalkBack television series *Demob*, but it was to prove a bit of a disappointment. Martin Clunes and Griff Rhys Jones starred as a couple of demobbed servicemen trying to make their way in post-war showbiz. It was the era of Tony Hancock and Peter Sellers so I felt very much at home. Unfortunately, most of my scenes were with Amanda Redman. She was a delightful actress but suffered an ectopic pregnancy during filming and was rushed to the Princess Margaret Hospital in Windsor. So most of our scenes were scrapped.

The production was unlucky all round. Dear Les Dawson, who was being brilliant as an old-time music hall comic, died before the shoot was over.

* * *

To raise funds for the Royal Marsden's 'Climb Your Own Mountain' charity appeal, I paid a visit to Number 10 Downing Street in 1991. My special project was to be a journalist for a day and I'd opted to interview Norma Major. I'd brought with me a long list of questions attached to a clipboard, but before I could get the first one out her husband, the Prime Minister, walked in. It was a Tuesday so he was just getting ready for Prime Minister's Question Time.

"Hello, Liz," he said. "I didn't know you were here."

When I explained that I'd agreed to interview a famous person for charity he said, "Gosh. Are you famous, Grub?"

What a lovely nick-name, I thought. I should have asked about it really, but instead I went straight into the first question on my list, which in retrospect was quite an embarrassing one.

"Mrs Cecil Parkinson and Mrs Paddy Ashdown stood outside their houses recently, holding hands with their husbands and saying that all was well after their spouses had had affairs. How would you react in the same circumstances?"

Well, of course, we all found out later that John Major was indeed having an affair at the time of this interview. In answer to the question she said that "public solidarity" was the important thing and that she would "almost certainly" forgive him. Then she laughed like a drain. But I *knew* she knew. Well, well, well…

It was a nice interview, and in the course of it I showed Norma a threatening letter I'd received for supporting the Tory party. I pointed out that the same thing rarely happened to Labour supporters like Vanessa Redgrave. ("Yuk," said Norma at the mention of the name.) We also discovered that Norma had failed the entrance exam for my school, St Saviour's and St Olave's Grammar School for Girls.

The Prime Minister looked at me and said, "You passed it, did you? Smartie Boots!" Then he headed off, saying to Norma, "I'll leave you with the difficult questions while I go off to answer the easy ones."

Another memorable charity event was organised by the Lord's Taverners and happened a bit earlier, probably in the mid-1980s. I was matched in a car rally against Stirling Moss and various other people. Each car had the driver's name displayed on it. A gallon of petrol was put into each car and the winner would be the one who had the most petrol left at the end of the race. The winner was to receive a case of the best champagne and the winning car was to be auctioned off in the evening.

Naturally, the organisers were anticipating that Stirling would be the winner, but it turned out to be me. Because they didn't want to auction a car with my name on it, they decided to move the goalposts and choose the car that had completed the race in the fastest time – which was Stirling's. I didn't even get the case of champagne!

* * *

I'd done a fair amount of radio over the years, co-starring with Fulton Mackay, Dinah Sheridan and others. Then in the late 1990s I did two series of *Truly, Madly, Bletchley*, playing opposite the show's writer, Julian Dutton, as a couple of local councillors who start up a cable radio station. I also appeared in an adaptation of the *Evening Standard* cartoon strip *Bristow*, with Michael Williams in the title role and Rodney Bewes as his right-hand man. Dora Bryan was in it too, as the tea lady, with Joan Sims and myself as the two charladies, Gert and Daisy. Sadly, Michael died soon afterwards of lung cancer.

Where television was concerned, I'd always been wary of making a long commitment to any one programme. I was offered *Coronation Street* many years ago but turned it down when told that if my character took off with the viewing public I'd be contractually bound to continue with it. I'd love to pop up in *EastEnders* or something but only as a peripheral character.

I appeared in *The Bill*, for example, because it was a lovely little self-contained episode that gave me the opportunity to actually murder someone, which delighted me. I did away with my lover and stashed him in the garden shed. I love all that wonderfully grotesque stuff and, thankfully, I was quickly found out and hauled away to prison, never to appear as that character again. My arresting officer, incidentally, was Kevin Lloyd, who was a fine actor but sadly died of alcoholism at only 49.

I presumably made a good job of the murder, though, because later on I was asked to play another murderer in *Doctors*. Roy Hudd was in that, and he's always a treat to work with. Our episode was all about variety comedians and light entertainment, a world we both know so well.

I suppose the only long-running show I might have liked to become a regular in was *Last of the Summer Wine*. That was a lovely show with beautiful locations and many old friends in the cast. Bill Owen, who played Compo for so long, died in 1999 and I was brought in for two episodes to play Compo's long-serving secret lover, Reggie Unsworth. I really loved the experience. There were lots of brass bands in Holmfirth, where the show was filmed, and they took me right back to the time before the war when my father took me out on Sundays.

In the programme itself, I had a few moments of emotion when I attended Compo's funeral and touched his coffin. I was also required to drive a tractor, and was given only a couple of hours in which to learn. I was sent to a car park to do so and just about mastered the basics. I had to drive poor Peter Sallis and Frank Thornton around and they had about as much confidence in my tractor-driving skills as I did. ("Don't drive too fast, Liz!") Frank was so relieved when he thought we'd done it – and absolutely horrified when our director, Alan J W Bell, called for another take!

* * *

By this time, of course, I was well aware that the Carry On films had become a national institution. So much so that in 1998 the National Theatre presented a highly regarded play about them called *Cleo, Camping, Emmanuelle and Dick*. Who would have thought that a play about the making of the Carry On films would be a hit at the National? But it was. Though if I'd been Valerie, Sid's widow, I'd have sued the playwright for libel.

I knew Sid very well for a very long time and I simply didn't recognise the person on stage. He was depicted as a dreadful old lecher, slobbering over a peach as if it were a vagina. So many books and dramas have appeared lately about the lives of Sid, Kenneth Williams, Tony Hancock, Hattie Jacques and others, it seems as if these old friends and colleagues of mine have become a national obsession. The majority of these plays and books are inaccurate and frankly unbelievable. People can misinterpret your life however they want once you're dead.

Those of us who haven't been buried yet are still whingeing about the fact that we never received any residuals for the Carry On films. But the person I really felt sorry for was Joan Sims, who appeared in the vast majority of the films.

We lived quite close to each other in Fulham at one time. She'd been in a large house but her agent advised her to sell it and move into a service flat instead. So Joan sold this huge house for peanuts; it would probably be worth about two and a half million now. Every seven years she'd have to renew her lease, and although she worked a lot – pretty much non-stop at one point – she never seemed to have any money. It was such a shame because she was a brilliant actress; in fact, I still think she was the cleverest of everybody in the Carry Ons and certainly the most versatile. Unfortunately, she did love her champagne and that doesn't come cheap.

There came a time when the lease on her flat was up and she had very little money. She also wasn't too well. So she swallowed her pride and wrote to Peter Rogers. She'd made all those films for him and had now decided to ask for some financial help. Peter wrote back and said "No." He was very sorry, he said, but it would set a precedent and therefore he couldn't help her. She was devastated.

A few of us rallied round to try and help her out. I'm more astute with financial matters than Joan was, so I'd go through her papers and say, "Look, you've got a pension here that you should have got when you were 60." So she cashed that in. I also noticed that she was always spending a fortune on taxi cabs, so I pointed out to her that there was a scheme in the borough she was in – Kensington – that allowed OAPs to take taxis for a pound.

I put her in touch with a whole group of people who helped her to cope, and also asked the Theatrical Benefit Fund to help her with the lease – which, thankfully, they did. But she'd put on a lot of weight by this stage and her legs were very bad. She died in 2001.

The public have a lot to be grateful to the Carry Ons for and I think Peter Rogers was very wrong in refusing to help Joan. I would've thought he'd have been glad to help. It was no more than she deserved.

CHAPTER FIFTEEN

Getting On

In 2002 I had first-hand experience of the despicable face of modern Britain. It isn't just a cliché – the streets really *have* become more dangerous. It certainly makes me nostalgic for the old London of my childhood.

One night I was walking Bracken Basset, my third Basset Hound, near my home in Fulham when I saw four youths approaching. Putting Bracken on his lead, I stood back against the wall to let them pass. Three of them did but the other one kicked Bracken, punched me, kicked Bracken again and then ran to catch up with the others. Then another of the boys turned back and ran towards me, gave me a running high kick on the thigh and booted Bracken into the street. He then hit me with a swinging punch, knocking out two of my teeth, and ran off laughing.

Four different households heard the commotion and dialled 999, but the police only arrived 15 minutes later. Two fresh-faced young constables turned up in a nice smart car and were very polite, asking if I needed an ambulance. I just wanted to get in the car and find the gang, but they'd long since disappeared. A week later I was still in shock. I was traumatised and had a huge bruise on my thigh and two teeth missing. Bracken had to be given two calming injections and was on tablets to reduce the swelling.

I'd been attacked near my home once before, and the police response had been just as slow and ineffectual then. Meanwhile, a police car was parked not 200 yards away, occupied round the clock by two officers in flak jackets, assiduously guarding none other than the disgraced ex-Cabinet minister Peter Mandelson. When I asked them whether members of the public could ever expect police protection, they just said "Write and complain." So I did, to the *Daily Mail*, and with good grace they went ahead and published my letter.

Later in 2002 I heard a break-in taking place at the home of my neighbour, the novelist Maureen Duffy. I immediately dialled 999 but was kept on hold while I stood at my doorstep watching the burglar and his female companion calmly walking out of Maureen's home, having kicked down the door. This recorded message droned on and on. I was kept in a queue on the telephone for several minutes. I couldn't believe it.

The girl was obviously acting as look-out; she just stood there with her arms folded and actually told me not to shout as I desperately tried to get through to the police. There was no panic for them – they obviously knew that the police would arrive long after they'd made their get-away. When the police did eventually turn up, they were on foot and angered me even further by saying they had insufficient resources to chase the burglars. They said they were very short-staffed and didn't have enough cars. They didn't even have enough money for petrol.

Maureen and I had contrasting political views, but we got on very well so long as we kept off the newspapers and just stuck to animals. (She's a vegan too, so even my leather handbags had to be kept out of sight!) In one by-election year, she proudly displayed an official poster for Fulham's Labour candidate, proclaiming in large letters that "Nick Raynsford lives here!" I was working on a TV show at the time and asked the art department to make up an alternative poster for me. It read "Thank God he doesn't live *here*!" I put it up in my window opposite and these two contrasting posters caused great amusement.

Kingsley Amis was one of Maureen's frequent visitors and, when he enquired about these two posters, she told him that "It's like living next door to Genghis Khan!"

* * *

Frustratingly, television producers these days don't take into account how experienced an actor you are. Generally this is because they've never heard of you, and the same applies to casting directors. So you have to read for them, and the most disconcerting thing about that is that they do the audition on film.

In 2006 I read for a TV film called *Pickles – The Dog Who Won the World Cup* and was cast as Camille Coduri's mum. I also acted opposite the dog of the title. I even had to bath him. Harry Enfield did the voice for Pickles, but that dog became a star in his own right, subsequently appearing in a very popular TV commercial in which he helped out around the house by doing the ironing and things. He's now Neil Dudgeon's sidekick in *Midsomer Murders* – and even *I've* never been in that show!

The year after that I read for a part in *Holby City*, playing a very ill old lady in bed. The engagement was for just two episodes and in the scene I read there was an attempt to resuscitate her at the end. This suddenly got me worried – the usual worry about getting contractually tied down to a show.

"She *does* die, doesn't she?" I asked, and I was assured that, yes, she did indeed pop off in the second of the two episodes.

Anyway, I got the part and did some acrimonious scenes with Sheila Steafel, who was playing my sister. And, yes, I watched myself die on the operating table with all these plastic things protruding out of me and bags of blood all over the place. The funny thing was that Edward Bennett, the director of that particular episode, couldn't stand the sight of blood and didn't actually watch those scenes being filmed.

Actually, I'm not sure if anyone at home was watching my big death scene either. I didn't realise it, but I was surrounded by three doctors in the scene, all of whom were embroiled in a love triangle. So the camera kept cutting to all the meaningful looks they were exchanging. They were also whispering these terribly significant lines over my dying body.

"Charming," I thought. "I'm bloody dying here and no one's paying the least bit of notice!"

* * *

Comic Heritage was founded by David Graham in the mid-1990s and I'd been asked along to several of their blue plaque events, honouring many of the comedy greats I'd worked with in the past. So I was delighted when David told me that the Heritage Foundation were going to honour me with a Liz Fraser tribute luncheon at the Grosvenor House Hotel.

It was March 2007 and my guests included Roy Hudd and June Whitfield, of course, plus Rolf Harris, Rick Wakeman, Jess Conrad, Vicki Michelle, Hayley Mills and Stanley Long. Phil Collins couldn't make it but sent a note that read

> Dearest Liz
> If there's one thing I miss about England, as well as the pubs, it's the opportunity I used to get to meet all my heroes and heroines at the Comic Heritage events. We had many a chat at those do's. You so richly deserve this tribute dinner. You've been such an icon of British comedy for as long as I can remember.
> Lots of love – Phil

Naturally I was very touched by all this and decided to make my speech that afternoon in verse.

Getting On

I'm making this speech completely in rhyme
A tribute for me? Well, it's just in time
Cos if they'd waited much longer
Instead of me looking back
I'd be up on the wall on a nice blue plaque

Now – how else would you know that it'd been me
In the first live play on ITV?
Or that for six months I managed to cope
Being in the very first ITV soap?

Jimmy Edwards' Matron in Whack-O!
Was again one of my early shows
In Dixon of Dock Green *when it went out live…*
Goodness, how did I ever survive?

But first there was drama school – it was the thing at that time
And I left with the Michael Redgrave trophy for mime
Rep in Accrington was my stage debut
For two pounds ten shillings – that's two pounds fifty to you

My first big stage break, then along came
A panto with Arthur Askey as Dame
I couldn't sing and couldn't dance
And got in the show completely by chance

I toured the country just about everywhere
When I see football results I think "I've been there!"
I did BBC 'extra' work for quite a long time
Then in The Tony Hancock Show *I had my first line*

How lucky I was to have been able to know
So many stars and work in their shows
Peter Sellers, Tommy Cooper, Benny Hill and Sid
What an experience for a fairly young kid

I'm All Right Jack *was a great break at last*
And oh my God what a wonderful cast!
I was nominated as one of the Best Newcomers of 1959
But there was another young star around at that time
Her name was Hayley Mills and she won that year
But look at us, Hayley – we're still here

I've made forty-odd films – in some I died
Shot three times and one suicide
Seven West End plays, one with Alastair Sim
What a privilege to work with him

Julie Andrews and James Garner in Hollywood – what a thrill!
And in The Family Way *I danced with John Mills*
Never worked with Michael Winner
But with Judy Garland I did *have dinner!*

Summer seasons were wonderful times
Knowing Roy Hudd when he was in his prime
He produced a variety act with my dog – very funny!
Didn't do it again – dog wanted too much money

Brian Murphy and I toured with Sweeney Todd *and were very good*
He sliced them up and I made the pud
For years I've worked on Variety Club committees
Oh, and last week I died in Holby City

I thank all my friends, and David, for today
To give me this chance to do it 'My Way'

Five years later, in April 2012, I was back at the Grosvenor for a Variety Club event in which I was made Celebrity Ambassador "for your endeavours towards sick, disabled and disadvantaged children and young people throughout the country."

All the former Chief Barkers were in attendance and I felt very proud.

I've worked on behalf of the Variety Club for, dare I say it, over 50 years now, going right back to the days when we helped thalidomide children in the early 1960s. I remain heavily involved, sitting on three committees – Variety at Work (arranging outings for handicapped children), the Appeals Committee of the Federation of Youth Clubs, and the Sunshine Coach Committee (visiting schools that apply for vehicles to check that they meet our criteria).

I currently have seven special needs schools in the borough under my wing, and I've been honoured to become something of a backstage auntie to lots of handicapped and under-privileged children. They've become part of my extended family and given me something to think and care about. I'd like to be remembered for this work just as much as for the world-famous Carry On films.

I'm also a Lady Taverner and work on behalf of the London Federation of Boys' Clubs. On top of that I'm a Lady Ratling. The gents had the Water Rats for so many years and I'd known and worked with numerous King Rats – Tommy Trinder, Ted Ray, Frankie Vaughan, David Nixon, Henry Cooper, Les Dawson, Davy Kaye, Roy Hudd, Melvyn Hayes, Danny La Rue and many more.

Not to be outdone, the Lady Ratlings were formed, though very few of the members are actresses. Most of them can sing, dance, perform rope tricks, do impersonations or dance the Can-Can at Christmas. I can't sing, dance, skate or play an instrument, but I do write a good letter!

* * *

In 2011 I attended a talk given by Bill Kenwright at the Jermyn Street Theatre. He'd filled out a little bit but it was a real delight to share his enthusiasm for the many shows he'd produced. I also hadn't realised how much work he'd done in his early days as an actor – cutting his teeth on *Coronation Street*, in fact.

Anyway, I sat there wondering if he'd ever know what a difference he'd made in my life. So many big things had happened to me while touring in his shows – the cancer, of course, and my brother's death. And it was through him, of course, that I'd started supporting Liverpool and became a very keen football fan.

The best thing, though, was seeing so much of our country. So many different towns and cities – museums, cathedrals, nightclubs, restaurants. Over the years I'd made friends north and south – and kept in touch with quite a few, even if only through Christmas cards. It was so nice to meet such a wide spectrum of our people in England, Scotland and Wales.

And it's all thanks to Bill.

Of course, when you're on tour you can't spend *all* your free time inspecting museums and cathedrals. You can also study the City columns in all the newspapers and get involved in stocks and shares. Well, I did anyway. I'd buy shares when they were first issued and on several occasions made a killing.

When I was in panto at Oxford in 1985 I bought 1,000 shares in Racal Electronics; they were £1.80 per share so it set me back £1,800. These then split (as shares do) and I received four Vodaphone shares for each Racal share and also shares in Chubb and Rentokil!

Another time I heard from my broker that shares in Wellcome were going like hot cakes so I wrote a cheque for £74,000. My bank manager had a fit but eventually agreed to honour the cheque with a stern "Don't ever do that again!" I received 2,000 shares at about £1.50 each. I eventually sold them for £14 per share.

This is how I made my money. My portfolio covered everything from health, electronics, killing rats and security companies to building firms, BP, Marks & Spencer and Sainsbury's. My ventures ranged from the very successful, such as Hackney and Hendon dog track, to the completely disastrous, like a lap-dancing club I set up with my friend Linda Regan about 15 years before they became fashionable.

This experience of the Stock Market helped me to buy properties that I'd then rent out. Two in Tooting, another in Elephant and Castle (that was going back to my roots), together with other properties in Fulham, Brighton and Bournemouth.

Being an actress never produced a large income, and as my work had mainly been in theatre and films I rarely received any residuals. Unless they become really big stars, people in showbusiness don't finish up with money. If I'd just had my career, full though as it was, I'd now be broke. So I'm very proud of my various financial dealings.

* * *

Nowadays, if ever I watch an old film of mine on television I always find that I'm the only one left alive. I sit there saying, "*He's* dead, *she's* dead... Oh my God, they're *all* dead."

I then reach over and switch off the TV while I still can!

With so many theatrical friends popping their clogs, I'm thankful that June Whitfield is, like me, still up and about. We see each other often; in fact, June is President and I'm Vice President of St Helier Hospital in Jersey, and we go over there annually to lend our support.

Nowadays I'm remembered mainly for the handful of comedy films I made in the 1960s and '70s, and of course I'm delighted that there are young people who watch all those old films and still like them, and write for photos. Though I don't talk very often about my old films, I have been coaxed into recording studios to do DVD commentaries for a few of them. Unfortunately, these sessions only reminded me that there are now so few of us left from that era. I did *Doctor in Love* with Leslie Phillips, but Terence Longdon, who was with me for the *Carry On Regardless* commentary, has since died. And *Carry On Cabby* I did all on my own. I was literally the only one left alive!

I've also been to a few autograph conventions recently, which can be great fun. "Excuse me," people say, "didn't you used to be

Liz Fraser?" Or "Can I please have your autograph? All the rest have gone!" I'm almost always signing ancient photos in which I'm posing with Sid or Peter or somebody. Occasionally someone comes along with a programme from *Oliver!* or *Sweeney Todd* or one of the other plays I did. In fact, if a fan letter mentions having seen me in a certain play in Manchester or wherever then I'll write a little note in reply. If I now get an influx of fan mail from people saying they saw me in a play in Manchester then I'll know they've read this book!

I still get plenty of letters (quite a few of them come from Germany, for some reason), and of course they normally include the same old pictures. But I am no longer that person in the photographs. In fact, I try not to look in mirrors too often. If it weren't for having to clean my teeth I'd put sheets over all of them.

Worse still is when I'm casually watching television and one of those *Legends* or *Heroes of Comedy* programmes pops up. They're all about Terry-Thomas or Benny Hill or Kenneth Williams, and there I'll be, blonde and bubbling and at least 50 years younger. It's tough getting old as a sex symbol.

Back in 1981 I worked with Chili Bouchier in the tour of *Murder Mistaken*. In her heyday in the 1920s and '30s she'd been a great beauty, the Mary Pickford of British silent cinema. I didn't know this when I first met her; to me she was just the lovely little old lady who was playing the maid.

But then people would turn up at the stage door and force photographs into her face. And there was Chili Bouchier in her youth, looking absolutely gorgeous. It took my breath away. She'd sign these photos for grateful fans but away from the stage door she sometimes became quite sad about it. I found it very moving.

We talked quite a lot. I discovered, for instance, that in the 1930s there'd been a big rivalry between Chili and Jessie Matthews, who was a huge star in British talkies of the day. In fact, Jessie had gone off with Chili's husband and Chili was very bitter about it.

Oddly enough, I'd previously had a brief encounter with Jessie too. I was living in Hatch End at the time and was just about to move to Fulham. I was in the midst of packing up all my belongings when I received a letter from Jessie, saying that she'd had a good career but the business seemed to have forgotten her. She was very lonely, she had no friends and she'd just heard that I was living in the area. She wrote, "I wondered if you'd like to come and see me and perhaps we could be friends."

I wrote back and said, "I'm ever so sorry but I'm moving and I won't be in the area any more." I deeply regret doing that to this day. I wish I'd said, "Oh, I'm moving actually but that doesn't matter. I'll come round and see you anyway." But at the time I had a busy career and life moved on very quickly. So I didn't.

Now, of course, there are blue plaques put up for people like Jessie Matthews. But for that kind of recognition you have to die first. You are of your time, then you go past your time. Then you die and become part of history.

But in the meantime I'm still here. I have the Hurlingham Club, bowls, bridge, stocks and shares, a pace-maker, my work for the Variety Club, a computerised car which I can't understand and, last but by no means least, Brodie Basset.

Sometimes, if I buy a 12-pack of toilet roll, I'll look at it and say, "This'll see me out!"

Actually, though, I'm determined to live until I receive a telegram from the Queen.

Unless, of course, she goes before I do...

APPENDIX

Stage, Screen and Radio

Note: The following chronology has been made as complete as possible, but bear in mind that, as early as 1959, estimates of Liz's television appearances already exceeded 100, many of them uncredited. Dates given refer to release (films), broadcast (television/radio) and opening nights (stage). Theatres mentioned are in London unless otherwise stated.

1952

Stage: Red Rose Players repertory season (ASM and small parts, including maid in *Jane Eyre*) – New Hippodrome Accrington, September to November

Stage: *Babes in the Wood* (chorus member) – Brighton Hippodrome from 24 December

1953

Stage: *One Way Traffic* (Jill) – tour, including Exeter 11 May, Tonypandy 18 May, Salford 22 June, Bilston 29 June, Lincoln 13 July, Scunthorpe 20 July, Leeds 27 July, Bromwich 3 August, Aston 31 August, Barrow-in-Furness 7 September, Wimbledon 14 September

Stage: *Cinderella* (chorus member) – Palace Theatre Leicester from 24 December

1954

TV: *The Grove Family* – unknown dates; series begins 9 April

Stage: *All-Girl Revue* – Grand Theatre Brighton from 21 June

Stage: *Woman of the Year* (Olga Johnson) – Embassy Theatre from 21 September

1955

TV: *The Benny Hill Show* – unknown dates; series begins 15 January

Stage: *Hot Water* (Rose Brown) – tour, including Westcliff 7 February, Norwich 21 February, Southsea 28 February; concludes May
TV: *Mick and Montmorency* – various episodes; series begins 30 September
Film: *Touch and Go* (girl on bridge) – October
TV: *The Geranium* (maid) – October (date unknown)
TV: *Sixpenny Corner* (Julie Perkins) – week beginning 26 December

1956

TV: *Sixpenny Corner* (Julie Perkins) – from 9 January; series concludes 1 June
TV: *The Tony Hancock Show* – series one (various episodes), 27 April to 1 June
TV: *The Dickie Valentine Show* – unknown episodes, 30 June to 4 August
TV: *Hancock's Half Hour* – series one: *'The Dancer'* (Teddy Girl) 3 August, *'The Bequest'* (Linda) 17 August
TV: *Great Scott – It's Maynard!* – 25 October
TV: *The Tony Hancock Show* – series two (various episodes), 16 November to 25 January 1957

1957

TV: *Dixon of Dock Green: 'False Alarm'* (Jeannie Richards) – 23 February
TV: *Jim's Inn* – unknown episodes; series begins 14 March
TV: *Hancock's Half Hour* – series two: *'The Alpine Holiday'* (autograph girl), 1 April
Film: *The Smallest Show on Earth* (girl in cinema) – April
TV: *Television Playhouse: 'Two Ducks on a Pond'* (Beryl, the maid) – 16 May
TV: *Shadow Squad: 'First Blood'* (Gilda) – two-part story, 17 and 20 June
TV: *Personal Appearance of Alan Young* – unknown episodes, 18 June to 10 September
TV: *The Army Game* – unknown episodes; series begins 19 June
Film: *The Shiralee* (chambermaid) – July
TV: *Whack-O!* (School Matron) – series two (all ten episodes), 1 October to 3 December

1958

Film: *Davy* (tea lady) – February
TV: *Dixon of Dock Green: 'They Don't Like Policemen'* (Maisie Perkins) – 15 February

Film: *Dunkirk* (factory worker) – March
TV: *Hotel Imperial: 'The Star in the Penthouse Suite'* – 22 April
Film: *Wonderful Things* (hot dog girl) – June
TV: *Educating Archie* – unknown episodes; series begins 26 September
TV: *Murder Bag: 'Lockhart Probes the Past'* – 29 October
TV: *Dixon of Dock Green: 'Strangers at the Same Table'* (Lena) – 15 November

1959

TV: *Hancock's Half Hour* – series four: *'The New Nose'* (girl in café) 16 January, *'Matrimony – Almost'* 13 February
Film: *Top Floor Girl* (Mabel) – May
Film: *Alive and Kicking* – June
Film: *I'm All Right Jack* (Cynthia Kite) – August
TV: *Hancock's Half Hour* – series five: *'The Economy Drive'* (canteen girl) 25 September
Film: *The Night We Dropped a Clanger* (Lulu) – October
Radio: *Hancock's Half Hour* – series six: *'The Picnic'* 20 October
TV: *No Hiding Place: 'Murder with Witnesses'* (Rose Glorie) – 18 November
Film: *Desert Mice* (Edie) – December
TV: *Play of the Week: 'Deep and Crisp and Even'* (Dora) – 22 December

1960

Film: *Two Way Stretch* (Ethel) – January
TV: *ITV Television Playhouse: 'Incident'* (Mavis) – 22 January
TV: *Hancock's Half Hour* – series six: *'The Ladies' Man'* (Muriel) – 15 April
TV: *Knight Errant '60: 'Beauty and the Feast'* (Gloria MacLean) – 3 May
Film: *Doctor in Love* (Leonora) – July
TV: *Citizen James* (Liz) – series one (six episodes), 24 November to 29 December
Film: *The Bulldog Breed* (NAAFI girl) – December
Film: *The Pure Hell of St Trinian's* (WPC Susan Partridge) – December

1961

Film: *The Night We Got the Bird* (Fay) – February
Film: *The Rebel* (waitress) – March
Film: *Fury at Smugglers' Bay* (Betty) – March
Film: *Carry On Regardless* (Delia King) – April
Film: *Double Bunk* (Sandra) – May
Film: *Watch it, Sailor!* (Daphne Pink) – August

Film: *Raising the Wind* (Miranda Kennaway) – September
Film: *On the Fiddle* (flower girl) – October

1962

Film: *A Pair of Briefs* (Gloria Hoskins) – March
Film: *Carry On Cruising* (Gladys 'Glad' Trimble) – April
Film: *The Painted Smile* (Jo Lake) – May
Film: *Live Now Pay Later* (Joyce Corby) – September
TV: *Citizen James* – series three, episode six: *'The Day Out'* ('guest star') 5 October
Film: *The Amorous Prawn* (Private Suzie Tidmarsh) – November

1963

Stage: *Next Time I'll Sing to You* (Lizzie) – New Arts Theatre from 23 January, Criterion Theatre from 18 February to 22 June
Film: *Carry On Cabby* (Sally) – June
TV: *Harry's Girls: 'Made in Heaven'* (Sally Witherspoon) – 29 November
TV: *No Hiding Place: 'Solomon Dancey's Luck'* (Sheba) – 23 December

1964

Stage: *Everybody Loves Opal* (Gloria) – tour, followed by Vaudeville Theatre from 1 April; closes 4 April
TV: *Fire Crackers: 'Fire Belle for Fire'* (Mary Medway) – 19 September
Film: *The Americanization of Emily* (Sheila) – October
Stage: *Don't Let Summer Come* (Margot) – Mermaid Theatre from 22 October

1965

Film: *Every Day's a Holiday* (Miss Slightly) – January
TV: *No Hiding Place: 'The Grass'* (Phyllis Nolan) – 29 March
Stage: *Meals on Wheels* (Dinah) – Royal Court Theatre, 19 to 29 May
Stage: *Too True To Be Good* (Nurse Sweetie) – Garrick Theatre; LF takes over from Dora Bryan on 22 November

1966

Stage: *Too True To Be Good* continues at Garrick Theatre; closes 29 January
TV: *The Avengers: 'The Girl from Auntie'* (Georgie Price-Jones) – 22 January
Film: *The Family Way* (Molly Thompson) – December

1967

TV: *Seven Deadly Virtues: 'A Pain in the Neck'* (Agnes) – 4 May
TV: *Mickey Dunne: 'Big Fleas, Little Fleas'* (Maisie) – 8 May

1968

Film: *Up the Junction* (Mrs McCarthy) – January
Stage: *The White Liars and Black Comedy* (Clea) – Theatre Royal Brighton from 5 February, Lyric Theatre from 22 February

1970

TV: *Randall and Hopkirk (Deceased): 'It's Supposed to be Thicker than Water'* (Fay Cracken) – 13 February
TV: *Tommy Cooper* – 21 April
Stage: *The Little Hut* (Susan) – New Theatre Bromley, 13 July to 1 August
TV: *Here Come the Double Deckers!: 'Starstruck'* (Zizi Bagor) – 3 October
TV: *The Benny Hill Show* – 28 October
TV: *The Goodies: 'Caught in the Act'* (Miss Heffer, Playgirl Club manageress) – 29 November
TV: *The Benny Hill Show* – 23 December

1971

Radio: *Parsley Sidings* (Gloria Simpkins) – pilot, 28 February
Film: *Dad's Army* (Mrs Pike) – March
TV: *ITV Sunday Night Theatre: 'Man and Boy'* (Countess Antonescu) – 6 June
Radio: *Parsley Sidings* (Gloria Simpkins) – series one, 5 December to 6 February 1972

1972

TV: *Jason King: 'An Author in Search of Two Characters'* (Claire) – 21 April
TV: *Crime of Passion: 'Lina'* (Denise) – 2 May
TV: *Albert!: 'If He'd Meant Us to Fly'* (Ann) – 30 May
TV: *These Two Fellas* – unscreened pilot, recorded 24 August
Film: *Hide and Seek* (Audrey Lawson) – October
TV: *Turnbull's Finest Half-Hour* (Faye Bush) – all six episodes, 17 November to 15 December

1973

Stage: *Rattle of a Simple Man* (Cyrenne) – Grand Theatre Leeds, from 9 July

Radio: *Parsley Sidings* (Gloria Simpkins) – series two, 29 September to 1 December
Stage: *Take Two at Bedtime* (Norah Wilcox) – Palace Theatre Westcliff, 9 to 20 October
TV: *Crown Court: 'Murder Most Foul'* (Lady Esham) – 27 December

1974

Stage: *Move Over Mrs Markham* – Pier Theatre Bournemouth, 13 May to 12 October
Stage: *Rattle of a Simple Man* (Cyrenne) – tour, including Ayr 28 October, Morecambe 4 November, Torquay 11 November, Darlington 18 November, Richmond 25 November, Wolverhampton 2 December, Wimbledon 9 December

1975

Film: *Three for All* (airport passenger) – May
Film: *Carry On Behind* (Sylvia Ramsden) – December

1976

Stage: *One of the Family* (Florrie Crump) – Forum Theatre Billingham 2 to 17 April then tour, including Coventry 19 April, Salford 26 April, Bournemouth 3 May, Bath 24 May, Richmond 7 June
Stage: *Carry On Laughing* (Milly) – Royal Opera House Scarborough, twice-nightly from 16 June; closes September
Film: *Adventures of a Taxi Driver* (Maisie) – July
Film: *Confessions of a Driving Instructor* (Mrs Chalmers) – August
Film: *Under the Doctor* (Sandra) – November
Stage: *Cinderella* (Fairy Godmother) – Richmond Theatre, December to January 1977

1977

TV: *She: 'Sight Unseen'* (Delilah Brown) – 24 April
Stage: *A Bedfull of Foreigners* (Helga Philby) – Duke of York's Theatre; LF takes over from June Whitfield; closes 11 June
Film: *Adventures of a Private Eye* (Violet) – July
Film: *Confessions from a Holiday Camp* (Mrs Whitemonk) – August

1978

Film: *Rosie Dixon Night Nurse* (Mrs Dixon) – February
Stage: *Donkey's Years* (Lady Driver) – tour, including Peterborough

3 April, Swansea 10 April, Worthing 17 April, Harlow 24 April, Sheffield 1 May, Darlington 15 May, Bath 19 June, Birmingham 17 July

TV: *Rumpole of the Bailey: 'Rumpole and the Alternative Society'* (Bobby Dogherty) – 10 April

TV: *Rainbow: 'Soft'* – 16 November

TV: *Robin's Nest: 'The Happy Hen'* (Vera) – 18 December

1979

TV: *The Professionals: 'Backtrack'* (Margery Harper) – 3 November

1980

Film: *The Great Rock 'n' Roll Swindle* (woman in cinema) – May

Stage: *Outside Edge* (Miriam) – tour, including Nottingham 9 June, Harlow 16 June, Hull 23 June, Swindon 30 June, Winchester 4 August, Stevenage 18 August, Cambridge 25 August

Stage: *Flare Path* (Countess Skriczevinsky) – Churchill Theatre Bromley, 24 September to 11 October

1981

Stage: *Murder Mistaken* (Freda Jeffries) – tour, including Bradford 2 March, Birmingham 9 March, Swansea 30 March, Leeds 13 April, Stevenage 20 April, Belfast 27 April, Bury St Edmunds 4 May, Eastbourne 11 May

Stage: *Fur Coat and No Knickers* (Edith Ollerenshawe) – tour, starting Crewe 13 July and including Manchester 27 July, Cambridge 17 August, Liverpool 7 September, Birmingham 21 September, Swansea 16 November

1982

Stage: *Fur Coat and No Knickers* (Edith Ollerenshawe) – second tour, including Leeds 25 January, Preston 1 February, Darlington 8 February, Reading 8 March

Radio: *Afternoon Theatre: 'Credit Account'* (Rita) – 29 January

Stage: *Fallen Angels* (Julia Sterroll) – tour, including Kirkcaldy 31 May, Lincoln 7 June, Hastings 14 June, Brighton 21 June, Chesterfield 28 June, Taunton 5 July

Stage: *Sweeney Todd* (Mrs Lovett) – tour, including Oxford 27 September, Taunton 4 October, Eastbourne 11 October, Richmond 1 November, Peterborough 15 November, Bath 22 November, Birmingham 6 December

1983

Stage: *Cinderella* (Fairy Godmother) – Gaumont Theatre Doncaster, 17 December to 7 January 1984

1984

TV: *Shroud for a Nightingale* (Mavis Gearing) – all five episodes, 9 March to 6 April

Stage: *Annie* (Miss Hannigan) – Belgrade Theatre Coventry, 2 to 27 October

TV: *Fairly Secret Army* (Doris Entwistle) – series one (episodes three to six), 5 to 26 November

1985

Stage: *Cinderella* (Fairy Story-Teller Flibberty Gibbet) – Apollo Theatre Oxford from 20 December

1986

TV: *Fairly Secret Army* (Doris Entwistle) – series two (all seven episodes), 1 September to 13 October

Stage: *Cinderella* (Fairy Godmother) – Civic Theatre Doncaster, December to January 1987

1987

TV: *Miss Marple: 'Nemesis'* (Mrs Brent) – second of two episodes, 15 February

TV: *Hardwicke House* (Agnes) – two episodes, 24 and 25 February (remaining episodes not transmitted)

Stage: *Oliver!* (Widow Corney) – tour, including Manchester 10 March to 18 April, Blackpool 16 June to 4 July, Bristol 7 July to 1 August, Norwich 4 to 15 August, Nottingham 18 to 29 August, Birmingham 1 to 19 September, Aberdeen from 6 October

1988

TV: *Rude Health: 'Green Paper'* (Mrs Joy) – 4 January

TV: *Eskimos Do It* (Mrs Dewey) – 3 August

1989

TV: *Capstick's Law* (Florence Smith) – 7 May

TV: *The Bill: 'Suffocation Job'* (Mrs Lester) – 11 May

TV film: *The Lady and the Highwayman* (Flossie) – 29 September

Radio: *Thirty-Minute Theatre: 'The Aquarium of Coincidences'* (Grace) – 10 October

1990

Film: *Chicago Joe and the Showgirl* (Mrs Evans) – July

1991

TV: *Birds of a Feather: 'Just Family'* (Olive Stubbs) – 21 September
Stage: *Cinderella* (Fairy Godmother) – Thorndike Theatre Leatherhead, 26 December to 18 January 1992

1992

Stage: *Alfie* (Ruby/the doctor) – Octagon Theatre Bolton, 6 to 28 November
Stage: *Aladdin and His Wonderful Lamp* (Empress of China) – Thorndike Theatre Leatherhead, 9 December to 9 January 1993

1993

TV: *Minder: 'How to Succeed in Business Without Really Retiring'* (Delilah) – 18 February
TV: *Demob* (Edith) – all six episodes, 15 October to 19 November

1994

TV: *The Bill: 'Good Days'* (Grace Walsh) – 7 July

1996

TV: *Wales Playhouse: 'Every Cloud'* (Nel) – 18 February

1997

Radio: *Truly, Madly, Bletchley* (Mrs Armitage) – series one, 29 January to 5 March
TV: *Drovers' Gold* (Ma Whistler) – 27 June

1998

Radio: *Afternoon Play: 'The Charm Factory'* (Violet) – four episodes, 21 to 24 September

1999

Radio: *Truly, Madly, Bletchley* (Mrs Armitage) – series two, 10 February to 17 March
Radio: *Bristow* (Gert) – series one, 21 April to 26 May; series two, 24 November to 15 December

2000

TV: *Last of the Summer Wine: 'Surprise at Throstlenest'* and *'Just a Small Funeral'* (Reggie Unsworth) – 30 April and 7 May
Radio: *Bristow* (Gert) – series three, 7 to 28 July

2006

TV Film: *Pickles – The Dog Who Won the World Cup* (Ada) – 3 June
TV: *Doctors: 'The Comedians'* (Beryl Gifford) – 11 December

2007

TV: *Foyle's War: 'Bleak Midwinter'* (Mollie Summersgill) – 11 February
TV: *Holby City: 'The Human Jungle'* (Tabitha Blackstock) – 24 May

Selected Personal Appearances

1958

TV: *This Week* – 17 April

1960

TV: *Star Parade* – unknown dates

1963

Stage: *D-Day with the Stars* – London Palladium, 6 June
Stage / TV: *Night of 100 Stars* – London Palladium, 18 July
TV: *Don't Say a Word* – 5 September

1964

TV: *The Celebrity Game* – 3 July
TV: *Don't Say a Word* – 3 September

1966

TV: *Juke Box Jury* – 30 April

1967

TV: *Call My Bluff* – 22 October

1968

Film: *Youth Wave* [includes 'making of' footage from *Up the Junction*]

1970

Radio: *Just a Minute* – 22 December

1971

TV: *The Des O'Connor Show* – 24 July
TV: *The World About Us: 'Under London Expedition'* (presenter) – 7 November

Appendix – *Stage, Screen and Radio*

1972
Stage: *Edwardian Music Hall*, Stevenage – 13 January

1974
Radio: *Does the Team Think?* – 11 June

1975
Radio: *Just a Minute* – 11 November

1976
Radio: *Just a Minute* – 3 February

1977
Stage / TV: *Night of 100 Stars* – Olivier Theatre, 5 June

1979
TV: *Give Us a Clue* – 2 January
TV: *Saturday Night at the Mill* – 24 February
TV: *It's a Celebrity Knockout* (contestant) – 29 August
Stage: *All Star Gala* – Alexandra Theatre Birmingham, 17 September
TV: *3-2-1* – 30 November

1980
TV: *Give Us a Clue* – 7 January
TV: *Looks Familiar* – 13 March
TV: *This is Your Life: Michael Aspel* – 14 May
TV: *It's a Celebrity Knockout* (contestant) – 11 July
TV: *Give Us a Clue* - 29 September

1981
TV: *It's a Celebrity Knockout* (contestant) – 31 August

1982
TV: *Give Us a Clue* – 13 April

1983
TV: *Movie Memories* – 1 January
TV: *Punchlines!* – 5 February

1985
Stage: *Gala: a tribute to Joyce Grenfell* – Aldwych Theatre, 20 January
TV: *Countdown* (Dictionary Corner guest) – six episodes, 6 to 13 February
TV: *Television Scrabble* – 5 and 12 July

1986
Radio: *The Press Gang* – 10 October

1988
TV: *Wogan* – 3 August

1990
TV: *The British Comedy Awards* – 16 December

1992
TV: *Kilroy: The Plight of the British Film Industry* – date unknown

1995
TV: *Surprise Surprise!* – 28 May
TV: *Heroes of Comedy: Terry-Thomas* – 17 November

1999
TV: *Collectors' Lot* – 31 March, 2 and 28 April

2000
TV: *The Unforgettable Sid James* – 4 December

2001
TV: *Can We Carry On, Girls?* – 5 September

2002
TV: *Heroes of Comedy: Sid James* – 23 February

2003
TV: *Boot Sale Challenge* – 6 March
Radio: *That Reminds Me – a lunchtime audience with Liz Fraser* – recorded 9 September

2005
TV: *The Unknown Hancock* – 26 December

2006
TV: *The Wright Stuff* – 28 March

2007
Radio: *The James Whale Show* – date unknown
TV: *British Film Forever: Sauce, Satire and Silliness* – 8 September
TV: *Breakfast* – 2 October

2008
Radio: *Stop Messin' About: A Tribute to Kenneth Williams* (presenter) – 12 April
TV: *Loose Women* – 4 July

Other personal appearances include *Pro-Celebrity Darts*, *Ultra Quiz*, *Pebble Mill at One*, *That's My Dog*, *The Zodiac Game*, *Vintage Quiz* and roving reporter on *GMTV*.

Index

Index

Index

Index

Index

Acknowledgements

Unless otherwise stated, all pictures are from the author's collection. We gratefully acknowledge the following additional sources:

Front cover and frontispiece
Portraits by Albert Clarke

Picture section one
Page 3: (top) *Davy* © Metro-Goldwyn-Mayer
Page 4: (bottom) and page 5: *I'm All Right Jack* © Studiocanal Films
Page 6: (top) *Desert Mice* © ITV Global Entertainment, (bottom) *Two Way Stretch* © Studiocanal Films
Page 7: (top left) *Two Way Stretch* © Studiocanal Films, (top right) *The Bulldog Breed* © ITV Global Entertainment, (bottom left) *The Night We Dropped a Clanger* © ITV Global Entertainment
Page 8: (top left) *Carry On Regardless* © Studiocanal Films, (top right) © Rex Features, (bottom) *Watch It, Sailor!* © Columbia Pictures Corporation

Picture section two
Page 1: (top right) *The Amorous Prawn* © British Lion-Columbia, (bottom) *Carry On Cruising* © Studiocanal Films
Page 2: (bottom right) *The Americanization of Emily* © Metro-Goldwyn-Mayer
Page 4: (top left) *The Avengers* © Canal +, (bottom) © Doug McKenzie
Page 5: (top left) *Man and Boy* © ITV Global Entertainment
Page 6: (bottom left) *Adventures of a Private Eye* © Salon Productions
Page 7: (top) © Doug McKenzie, (inset) © Doug McKenzie
Page 8: (bottom) © Doug McKenzie

Any errors or omissions will be corrected in future editions.

The publishers also wish to thank: Dick Fiddy (British Film Institute), David Pratt, V&A Department of Theatre and Performance, Stephen McKenna (www.tpmckenna.com) and the Palace Theatre Club Archive (Palace Theatre, Westcliff on Sea).